The Best of

Living
at
YES!

Sharon Marquart

Dedicated to the Spirit that gives us life!
Thanks for your loving inspiration and guidance.

Blessings to those who guide me from the world of Spirit.
My beloved companion, Peg Gearhart
My parents, Ralph and Ruby
My Grandma Marquart
A host of others

Blessings to my supportive network of friends
who keep me grounded and focused.

Blessings to all those who call Divine Wisdom through me
in our coaching sessions, classes and workshops.

Blessings to the editors for their hard work in
making my words come alive on paper.

Blessings to you for opening this book.
May your life be changed!

Table of Contents

Introduction

Renew Your Sense of Purpose

As the Earth renews itself with the arrival of spring, it's a great reminder to refresh yourself by renewing your sense of purpose. I took a moment to recently reflect, renew and rediscover my own sense of purpose and was reminded once again of just how blessed I truly am to have discovered and live my life's passion.

As I look back over the past 3 years of Living at YES!, I am very excited at the many lives – including my own - that have been touched, awakened and changed. Living at YES! became official on March 14, 2005. It's exciting to realize so many wonderful things have happened in such a very short time.

The idea actually came to me in a dream. I woke up one day with the words "Living at YES!" on my mind. "What a great phrase!," I thought. "What am I supposed to do with this?" The next night before going to sleep, I asked, "What does Living at YES! mean?" I awoke with this answer: "Living at YES! is your new mission, purpose and profession. Although I had been practicing as well as teaching others to live this way of life for the past 15 years, I had never officially given it a name. That night in my dream, all the pieces finally "fit".

YES stands for "You Embracing Spirit." WOW! Living at You Embracing Spirit! What a great title! I was thrilled and suddenly flooded with ideas and possibilities for this new coaching program I was to create. I thought of little else for weeks. I allowed it to sink into every crevice of my thinking process, because I knew that when the Universe gave me a gift as rich as this, my life would change forever. And it has.

I had a similar experience in 1996 when I was traveling and presenting workshops and teaching metaphysics. I was getting an 800-telephone number when the operator asked me the name of my business. Out of my mouth, without a single thought passing through my mind, popped "Open Heart Ministries". I soon realized that OHM is a name for God!

From this moment on, I knew my heart had made its commitment to be a messenger of love from the Universe to the world. OHM's mission statement is "Raising Spiritual Self-Esteem in a human World." OHM has now become my Wedding Ministry offering Non-Denominational/Interfaith wedding ceremonies. I felt the same sense of clarity and purpose when the dream came to me that night. I knew this was the next step in my life's journey of helping others live a life in full abundance.

Over this past year our (The Universe and I) website has been created to share our expansive philosophies on life. Our graphic artist helped create our logo with the "Y" in the shape of a heart. When you "Live at YES!", your heart opens. More than 3,000 people receive the weekly inspirational message with more signing up each week. Our editor has interviewed and written the stories of members who shared their "Personal Success Stories" in hope of inspiring others. It's working!

In 2006, we began the yearlong program, "Embrace Your Magnificent Self" that is proving to be a wonder-filled opportunity for participants. We are also beginning the Entrepreneurial Spirit Groups for self-employed business owners creating businesses from the heart. I have also facilitated tele-classes, held on the first Thursday of the month, with participants from across the USA and as far away as Hong Kong.

Most importantly, I have been blessed to do what I do best: Life Coach. I have the opportunity to coach many people in releasing their fears, removing self-imposed obstacles and in embracing the spirit of life!

As I reflect on the past year of Living at YES!, I feel so very blessed by all the people's lives I have been able to touch by encouraging them to discover their heart's desire and courageously embrace their visions. I am so grateful that we can all have what I call, "A working relationship with the Universe".

I renew my purpose to open my heart to Wisdom and bring metaphysical and theoretical Truth into everyday, practical language. Thank you for Living at YES! and for sharing the journey with me.

As you mow your lawn and plant your gardens this spring, I invite you to contemplate renewing **your** sense of purpose and to rediscover your sense of adventure as you continue on your life's journey.

Starting Anew

Clarity, Confidence and Conviction

The beginning of a New Year--be it a calendar year, a birthday or a new phase of your life--feels the same as when I begin a new journal. All the pages are fresh and blank inside a beautiful bound book, ready to be filled with the adventures of my life. This feeling is both exciting and full of anxiety as I anticipate the unfolding of this New Year. The one thing I know is that I have taken my finger off the pause button and am ready to live full-out! How about you?

Have you set your intentions for the year? Have you begun to have clarity in what you want to create for the year? OR, is your life still on hold waiting until you know exactly what it is you want? Are you answering, "Um...maybe, I don't know, let's wait and see." How many times have you heard yourself offer this response? Did you realize that these responses are much like pushing the "hold" button to experiencing life? Your life is on hold when you are not living at "yes"!

"Living at YES!" means you live your life full-out. You are open to possibilities, to opportunities. It means you live your life with *Clarity, Conviction and Confidence*. "Living at YES!" means you have learned how to enjoy the present moment and that you embrace all that life has to offer. You have become more fully empowered, allowing life to unfold before you with ease.

"Living at YES!" does not mean that you say, "yes" to everything that comes your way. When you live at "yes" you are empowered to say "no." There is a verse in the Christian Holy Book that says, "Let your yea be yea and your nay be nay." In other words, be clear in your choice.

Clarity

Living in the power of choice means that you are not a victim to life's circumstances. When you know you have a choice, you are living in freedom. In order to be clear on your choice, you are first acknowledging that you *have* a choice.

"I don't know" and "maybe" are phrases of doubt. When you live in the energy of doubt, you are shut down to life. Once shut down, you soon begin to lack the confidence necessary to take the next step moving you forward into your life. -and doubt soon grows into fear.

Living in doubt and fear can soon become paralyzing. Once paralyzed, choice is not an option and you feel like a victim. When you live your life as victim, life responds by creating more circumstances that support you feeling like a victim. The life force energy, now being cut off from its natural flow, will begin to be reflected in your health, your relationships, your physical body *and* in you wallet. You may begin to experience stiff joints, a decrease in your cash flow and an increase in your waist size. You may begin to experience stress in your relationships and just too many hard days at the office.

Living in doubt is like having a hidden virus in your computer, the invisible bug that has been slowly creeping its way into your files, contaminating them. You only notice it when you realize you have become locked out and unable to access what you need.

Life offers us basically two choices. One choice is to repel life and the other choice is to embrace life. We are either embracing or repelling. When you live in doubt, you are actually making the choice to push life away. Ironically, what we are pushing away is what we want to experience most.

I once heard someone say that when we say, "I don't know," we are really saying, "I am too afraid to take any action; I am too afraid to take the next step towards embracing life." "I don't know" is really a response that signifies that one is shutting down.

Moving forward with Confidence
A survey by a Harvard psychologist showed there are two things that make people happy. One is that they know exactly what they want - clarity; and two, they know they were moving towards getting it – *confidence.* Life feels great when you realize your goal and know you are confidently moving towards it. What is confidence and what gives someone confidence?

Confidence is having a feeling of trust within yourself. When you live with confidence, you are feeling good about yourself and you trust that you will respond to life's situations in an empowering way. Like self-esteem, confidence grows as you place your awareness onto it. Every action you take that you can feel good about, every step forward that you take, even when feeling the fear and doing it anyway, builds your levels of confidence. Confidence builds as you build your confidence; one experience at a time.

When you live in the energy of doubt, you are shut down to life. Once shut down, you soon begin to lack the confidence necessary to take the next step, moving you forward into your life. Doubt soon grows into fear. Living in doubt and fear can often become paralyzing. Once paralyzed, choice is not an option and you feel like a victim. When you live your life as victim, life responds by creating more circumstances that support you feeling like a victim. The life force energy is being cut off from its natural flow.

In the movie, <u>The Secret</u>, Jack Canfield offered the following analogy. "You can drive from NY to CA in the dark with your headlights shining only 200 feet ahead of you." Once you have clarity, you can take the next right step towards your goal with confidence. You put yourself in the natural flow of the life energy force trusting that you will know what to do next. Your level of confidence builds each step of the way.

Remember that we are all a little unsure when we try something new. Our confidence may get rattled a bit, but when you can step back and sit in your clarity, you recommit with conviction.

Conviction

The word conviction means having a strong persuasion or belief. I heard this word frequently spoken in a former religious setting. It would be common to hear someone say they have a strong conviction for Christ. Meaning, they have a strong belief, they are convicted, in the teachings of the religion. Let's take the word conviction out of the religious context. What are your convictions?

In the core of you, what are your beliefs? When you examine your core, what is the Truth that lies deep within you? My studies in metaphysics have taught me the importance of knowing what I believe. I learned that my beliefs are the basis of how I interpret my life's experiences. How I view and respond to my life's experiences is based on what I believe. My beliefs are formed by the thoughts I have, which are fueled by my emotions.

What strong beliefs do you have? What perceptions of the world do you hold firmly as your Truth? When we came into this world, we entered free of thinking. We were just busy having fun. Then, as time passed, we were programmed and trained on how to perceive and respond to the world.

At the beginning of this series, I stated that "Living at YES!" means you live your life full out. You have learned to enjoy the present moment and you embrace all that life has to offer. When you examine your beliefs, do they empower you to live in full expression? Do your beliefs allow you to stretch your comfort zone?

Empower yourself to stop and explore the beliefs that hold you back, that keep you from really being who you are and doing what you are meant to do in this lifetime. Empower yourself to live with strong conviction and to make the necessary changes from the inside out.

Make it a priority in your life to live with **Clarity, Confidence and Conviction**.

Live at YES!

Breaking Bad Habits

I'll let you in on a little secret. Habits cannot be broken!

Stop feeling frustrated and stop criticizing yourself for not being successful at breaking that bad habit you've been stuck in for years. Habits cannot be broken...they can only be **changed**.

Habits are energy patterns created through repetition. We create habits to help us establish a familiar world, and then rely on them to help us feel in control. We have many habits that move us through our day.

We categorize our habits as either "good" or "bad". For instance, we usually begin our day with a series of morning habits. Waking at the same time, stopping off at the bathroom, brushing our teeth, taking a shower, getting dressed, eating breakfast, taking the same route to work, stopping in the coffee shop for a familiar brew, etc. We would probably label these habits as "good habits". They are the habits that positively *support* us in beginning our day.

In contrast, the habits that *sabotage* us from living a healthy and balanced life, we label "bad". Let's say in our daily morning rituals we've developed a "bad habit" of hitting the snooze alarm one too many times, causing us to rush through our morning in haste rather than relaxation. What makes this habit "bad" is it does not support us in feeling balanced as we begin our day.

How do you break a "bad habit"? The first step in breaking a bad habit is to stop *trying* to break it and create a plan to **change** it. Next, identify a habit that sabotages you living your best life. Ask yourself "What good habit can I replace it with that would be most supportive in my living a balanced life? Create a plan to shift your energy from a sabotaging pattern to a supportive pattern. In this scenario, you could choose to set the alarm earlier so you can continue to hit "snooze" and wake up slowly; you could move the clock further away from the bed so you have to get up to turn it off; or you could purchase another alarm clock without a snooze button. What a simple solution! Once we look at the situation in a different light, we realize we have many choices that support us in living a fulfilled, balanced life.

What a wonderful wake-up call!

Change Brings Choice

Some time ago, I wrote a two part weekly inspiration on becoming unstuck and moving through change. I offered an opportunity for you to look at the attitudes that support you in staying stuck and attitudes that support you moving through change.

A big change we are all currently experiencing is the arrival of spring! Most of us change the time on our clocks, causing the loss of an hour of sleep. The positioning of the sun changes the hours of daylight and the daily temperature. It is a change that happens every year--and a change most people look forward to--not because of the loss of sleep, but because it provides a new outlook on how we view each day. How refreshing it is to wake to a sunrise, blossoming trees and birds singing vs. dark, bleak and silent winter mornings. Although we may resist change in our personal lives, most people are enjoying the seasonal changes and are looking forward to the new choices these changes bring.

Choice can be defined as, "Making a selection; the opportunity or power of choosing." Realizing that you have choices expands your energy and offers you new opportunities to experience life in a different way. For me personally, I am very aware of the new choices that come with the arrival of spring. For example, I have more choices in my life planned to fully embrace the spirit of health and wholeness. I have new choices in the time of day I exercise. I have the choice to do my workout indoors at the gym or outdoors surrounded by the beauty of nature. Choosing an outdoor activity creates even more choices. Taking a walk and riding my bicycle are two of my favorite outdoor activities. If I choose my bicycle, do I take a short ride alone or a longer ride with a friend? Am I up to a ride with hills, a flat ride along the riverfront or a healthy mix of both? Each choice brings me a different level of satisfaction.

As you become aware of the new choices the change of season brings, consider the new choices that become available to you when you make a change in your life. Remember, change is a given in life. Unconscious change happens regardless of whether we're ready or not: Seasons change, our appearance changes, our relationships with ourselves and with others change. Life and change are one.

Conscious changes are choices we make, like choosing which activity to include in our daily exercise program. Our bodies are going to change with time, but choosing how we care for our bodies is completely up to us. Conscious change does not always come easily or naturally, and we tend to resist that which is not comfortable.

When you are ready to make a conscious change in your life and you begin to feel your resistance, take a moment to consider instead how these new choices can empower you to live life in full abundance! This season, be inspired to "Spring Forward" so you can embrace these choices as gifts that will keep you physically, spiritually and emotionally healthy from one season to the next.

Having Fun Manifesting

For many years I've been teaching, speaking and coaching about how we create our own reality by the way we think. Since the release of the DVD "The Secret", there has been more conversation about creating and manifesting your reality. From several articles I've read in USA Today and many web blogs, the question often comes up about manifesting things for personal use versus manifesting things for the world at large. And the question from Spiritual groups comes in, "Where is God in all of this?" This week I would like to share my thoughts about this topic.

Our human experience involves collecting "things" and having things that make life easier and more pleasurable. It is true that most of us in the civilized world have more things than we need. We collect and store and recycle and throw away our things. Our things can help to give us an identity. It is unfortunate that having things can also become an attempt to fill up an internal emptiness.

When someone is struggling to pay the bills, keep the car running, find and maintain a healthy relationship or struggle through an illness, they can feel un-empowered and sometimes victimized. If you are feeling powerless, it is exciting to claim your power by learning to create things.

We have two options. One is to use our thoughts and emotions to focus on, claim and declare what we DON'T want. You know the saying, "the squeaky wheel gets the grease". When something is *not* working in our life, it becomes the squeaky wheel getting our attention.

The second choice is to use our thoughts and emotions to claim what we DO want, regardless of what life looks and feels like in the present moment.

In exploring these choices, I am excited as a life coach and teacher of metaphysics to support someone truly moving into living their power and learning how to manifest things. What better way to learn how to create than to be in need, in someway, and change your thinking and feelings. This gives you a visual of how to change your life around. When you practice creating things you need in life, you become powerful and go from a place of struggle to a place of serenity. When you are no longer struggling, and instead are feeling more empowered in creating your own reality, then you can move onto joy. And then we can have fun and joy in creating more things to experience. This joy opens us up and once opened, it is natural to share your joy with others. And this is where God is located, in the joy we share with others.

Learning to claim our personal power by creating our lives makes us feel good and connected and naturally progresses into sharing joy with others. Be inspired this week to create in joy and share your joy with those around you.

Making up Stories

Author Lisa Nichols says, "We use our stories to keep us where we are." I started thinking, how else could we use our story?

Each and every day we make up a story about our life. We make up stories all day long about everything that happens in a day. Some of the stories we make up are about mundane events of the day. Some are charged with excitement about something new or unexpected that has happened. And then there are the stories we make up that scare us half to death. We have the variety of nightmares, dramas, "the whoa is me" the "who done it" and of course the all too familiar "ain't it awful" story lines. The way we tell the story is based on how we perceive the events. Our perceptions are based on the beliefs we hold in our memory bank.

What kind of stories did you tell in the conversations you had today? And yes, I know, things *have* happened to you. Keep in mind the wisdom from the sages, "It's not what happens to you, it is what you do with what happens to you." We have the power to use our stories to keep us where we are or we can become empowered to tell stories that will take us where we want to go. When you empower yourself with this knowledge you begin taking steps to wake up from your own nightmares, to free yourself.

Here is a fun way you can begin to tell your stories in a new light. When you catch yourself telling a story that is tragic, stop. Remind yourself there is another way to tell the story.

Shift your perception:

- Tell the story from the other person's perspective.
- Tell the story as if it were the saddest tale you have ever heard.
- Tell the story as if it were the funniest thing that ever happened.
- Tell the story with no emotion whatsoever.

Telling the story from these different perspectives will help you disengage from your current perspective and shift your energy.

Everything that happens to you in a day becomes your story. Empower yourself to tell the story differently. Observe how the events of your life will also begin to shift.

Change your perception, change your story, and change your life. Make up stories that get you where you want to go. Make up stories of who you want to be. Make up stories that allow you to feel good about your life.

Use Your Power of Intention to Imagine Your Day

When you jump into your day unconsciously, most of your energy is used *reacting* to what happens "to you". This constant reacting is draining and can soon lead to burnout.

On the other hand, when you set an intention at the beginning of each day, you are consciously focusing your thoughts towards a desired direction....intentionally. By setting your intention daily you take *action* that can prove to be a powerful tool in creating a day that makes you feel good about your life, your self-esteem, your interactions with others, your sales etc.

As soon as you wake up, maybe when the alarm goes off but you're not quite awake, or maybe when you are in the shower, begin to think about your day ahead. Here are some questions that can be helpful:

- How will your energy be today?
- What's your mood?
- How are you in your body?
- What are your food choices?

Imagine your energy flowing evenly and balanced throughout the day. You feel good in your body and clothes. When you're hungry you choose food that recharges and refreshes you. Imagine your commute to work as a cool, easy ride with the perfect flow of traffic, great music on the radio and your arrival on time.

- What appointments are on your calendar?
- What are your expectations of the day?
- What's on you schedule?

- If you are in sales, how are your sales flowing today?
- How will your important meeting flow?

You can set your intention at the beginning of every day, and throughout the day. If you are not able to visualize, try journaling. If you can't journal, speak your intentions out loud.

Use the power of intention to imagine your day!

Pivotal Points

As You Choose

"Ancient Spiritual traditions remind us that each moment of the day, we make the choice to either affirm or deny our lives. Every second, we choose to nourish ourselves in a way that support or depletes our lives, to breathe deep and life-affirming breaths or shallow, life-denying ones, and in a manner that is honoring or dishonoring."

Gregg Braden - The Diving Matrix

Look around you. Your life right now is the reflection of the choices you have made up until now. It is only when you live in a victim consciousness that you believe you had no choice. As the victim, you focused on what was happening "to you" rather than how you can make life happen "by you".

The most empowering tool you have in creating a wonderful human experience in this adventure we call LIFE, is to remember that each moment you are at "choice point". Each moment you have a choice about how you want to perceive the situation, you have a choice about what you want to believe about it, and you have a choice about how you want to respond. All these choices are within your power.

You may know someone or heard about someone or read about someone in a book or magazine that took a tragic situation and turned it into a positive one. You remember it because it inspired you. And you prayed that you never have to experience such drama. You don't have to wait until a major event reminds you that you have the ability to make choices. You can begin each day consciously choosing how you want to live and create your life.

As your life unfolds a tapestry is created. It is by the choices you make that your tapestry weaves itself together in the form of either a beautiful design or a tangled mess. Your choices direct the flow and blend of patterns. Be mindful to create your life's colorful tapestry by personally choosing your design and patterns.

There was a time in my life when I was caught up in a tangled web of defeating choices. I made choices that created drama and painful situations that kept me feeling powerless. I played out the "martyr" archetype and attracted people and situations that would give me a stage to show what I was made of. I played out the martyr so well that I could have been nominated for an Academy Award! I seriously wove martyr into all areas of my life while complaining how badly life was treating me.

My turn-around came when I learned that I had the power to choose. I quickly and steadily untangled myself from the mess of a life I had created and began to weave choice into every day.

Here is an idea you can use to remind yourself how to use your power of choice to create a beautiful life. When you first wake up in the morning, perhaps in your morning prayers, meditation or maybe when you are in the shower, visualize walking through your day. Set your day up energetically before you even walk out the door. Create an energetic pattern of you making powerful choices well in advance. Then, as the day unfolds begin to consciously align yourself with those choices. You can begin with the small choices you decide each day. Begin by choosing consciously. For instance, imagine your commute to work. There may be a particular intersection that has a long traffic light. What are you going to do as you sit and wait? What are your choices? What will you choose to think about? When you arrive at work, how will you choose to greet co-workers and approach your work for the day? Write the word "choice" on a piece of paper and place it visibly in front of you. When frustration begins, glance at the paper and remind yourself that you are at "choice point". Take a deep breath, a life-affirming breath, and then choose your response.

Every day, consciously breathe deep, life-affirming breaths that support you in living your best life. Weave a beautiful tapestry that you can be proud of and sure about. Honor your life and fill it with joy and delightful experiences. Celebrate in your creations!

Balancing Your Energy Bank Account

Have you balanced your *Energy* bank account lately? Did you even realize you had one? Since life itself is energy, each one of us has an **Energy Bank Account**! All of life is about investing and receiving *Energy*. And just as you can become more financially abundant when you make wise investments with your money, you can become *Energy* abundant when you make wise investments with your *Energy*.

Much of your *Energy* is invested in earning and spending money. Your *Energy* is transformed into money, which in turn is deposited in your bank account. You go to work where you transform physical *Energy* into money *Energy*. Money *Energy* is then transformed into the goods and services that you need and desire. Look around your home. All that surrounds you is a reflection of your ability to transform your life's *Energy* into the things that bring you physical comfort.

With money *Energy*, when you make wise investments, you build your financial account; when you make unwise investments, you deplete that account. Why do you think we call unwise choices, "poor" choices? You would never make a financial investment in a product that **charged** you interest, right? And yet, you will make investments in activities that do just that when they deplete your *Energy* bank account.

Poor investments are things like eating food that drains you energetically; choosing to sit and vegetate rather than taking a brisk walk; "spending" time with people who drain you, worrying or feeling anxious about past or future events, feeling too afraid to risk doing something you love, then beating yourself up about it. Even having clutter in your home slows your *Energy* flow and costs you *Energy* when you spend unnecessary time searching for something. These are just a few examples of the activities that are charging you interest on your *Energy* investments. These poor investments are bound to deplete your *Energy* bank account.

Increase your *Energy* bank account by making wise *Energy* investments. You know how to discern what is a poor investment and what is a wise investment. The key to building your *Energy* bank account is to balance your account often. In fact, you can do this on a daily basis. Check in with yourself at the end of the day. Did you make *Energy* investments in the things that paid you interest, nurtured you and supplied you with an abundance of energy?

We are all here to be ***Energy* Abundant**! It's just a matter of making wise *Energy* investments in ourselves. When we place value and invest in ourselves, the abundance will begin to flow nonstop!

Moving Through Change

Part One - 9 Attitudes that Keep You Stuck

Have you become proficient at "managing stuck"? Have you given up on "plan A, B, C and D, abandoning dreams of what you *thought* your life would be like? Are you stuck in managing stuck?

Picture this: you're in a rowboat anchored in the middle of a river. You watch as objects floating down the river pass you by. When it rains, you put up a tarp. When the current changes, you keep your paddle in the water so you don't tip over. When a log comes your way, you swing the boat around. Pulling up anchor and heading around the next bend in the river or going ashore requires more energy than you think you have. All your energy goes into "managing stuck"?

The Truth is, change IS going to happen. Change is a part of life. Staying stuck is NOT going to make change from happening. Here are nine attitudes that may be keeping you stuck.

1. You do not believe you deserve or are entitled to something different or better than you have.

2. You have negative thoughts about yourself and in your ability to change. Making a change may be too embarrassing, too hard, or it's always the wrong time.

3. Life is chaotic. In the past problem solving creates chaos. Making plans to change become elaborate raising your level of anxiety. When you feel overwhelmed with anxiety, you shut down.

4. You feel alone. You lack a support system to help you clarify a plan and to feel connected with others as change happens in your life.

5. You are a perfectionist. If you are unable to come up with the "perfect" plan, than no plan will work.

6. You make the same choices over and over without seeing results so you stop.

7. You lack a sense of identity within yourself. Your identity of yourself is in your relationships, the roles you have, your education and external conditions.

8. You feel guilty about how making a change in your life will affect others.

9. You are so proficient at managing stuck that any change takes you too far outside your comfort zone.

Do any of these nine attitudes sound familiar? The good news is that when you **recognize** you're stuck, you have **already** begun to get unstuck.

Moving Through Change

Part Two - 9 Attitudes That Support You in Moving Through Change

The Truth is, change IS going to happen. Change is a part of life. Staying stuck is NOT going to keep change from happening.

In Part One I gave you nine attitudes that may be keeping you stuck. When you are willing to give up "managing stuck" here are nine attitudes that will support you in moving through change.

1. You have a clear sense of Self, with a capital "S". You have an intimate relationship with our inner soul.

2. You have confidence in solving problems as they arise. You have developed the ability to see above the problem to discover the solution.

3. Your personal identity is not in success or fail. Failures = feedback.

4. You strengthen your ability to change because you are able to build on your past successful changes.

5. You know that not changing is no option. Change equal evolving, evolving is good.

6. You know how to invest your life's energy in creating a life that rich and full.

7. You have a solid support system that gives you honest feedback and "will hold the space" for you as you move through change.

8. You have a sense of adventure and you are okay with playing outside the comfort zone.

9. You believe in a Divine Purpose and a Divine Plan for your life.

When you begin to realize that you are stuck in your life, and make a commitment to change, begin to embrace these nine attitudes that will support you through the process of change.

Make up Your Mind!

How do you want to experience your day? Well, "make up your mind" and do it now! It is all up to you. The world you experience each day is based on how you choose to **perceive process** and **respond**. You are in total control of how your day will be experienced!

Notice I did not say you were in charge of how **others** are going to behave or how the events of the day will flow. You are in control of how you will perceive and respond to your day's events and the people that make them up. And you can make that choice before you even begin your day!

It will be helpful for you to create a time at the beginning of your day when your conscious mind awakens to your outer world to get yourself connected to your inner self, your soul or whatever you choose to name it. As soon as you open your eyes in the morning or have your first cup of coffee, your conscious mind begins connecting to the visible world. Take a few moments to just sit, relax and breathe. Take this time to "mentally walk through your day".

This is the time to use your conscious thinking to "make up your mind" about how you will experience your day. For the most part, you already know how, when and where you will be traveling; you know what's on the day's calendar of events and you generally know with whom you will be encountering and what task you will be accomplishing. "Make up your mind" about **how** you will be experiencing your day. How will you **emotionally** approach each of these tasks?

How do you choose to feel as you travel to your day's commitments? How do you choose to feel as you accomplish your day's tasks? How do you choose to feel about the conversations you have throughout the day? Use your imagination to envision all the possibilities your mind can possibly hold. "Make up your mind" about how you will feel as you experience your day.

"Make up your mind." Doing this daily exercise is a fundamental key to living a joyous and meaningful life. Face it, most of your day is spent observing and analyzing if you are safe. Yes, safe. You want to feel safe and secure as you experience life. In order to do so, you need to keep your radar open and working to constantly feed you information so you can build your walls or design your battle plan! Securing walls and battling will wear you out; and even more important, rob you of the opportunity to truly experience your life!

How do you want to experience your day? Well, "make up your mind" about it right now! It is all up to you.

Achieving Inner Peace

You mean you have to <u>Work</u> to achieve Inner Peace?? You mean it doesn't come natural? You betcha!

For most of us, our waking hours are focused on *reacting* to what is happening in the world outside ourselves. The many activities, the never-ending lists to complete, all the interactions with others can cause us to be tense, worried and anxious. And if you are a parent, your responsibilities are often doubled or tripled. This constant state of "don't blink or we'll miss something" hypersensitivity can be very tiring and leave us feeling anything but peaceful! Whew! The chaos that can accompany everyday living explains why we have to put forth extra effort to achieve inner peace.

First we must take responsibility that <u>we</u> are in control of our thoughts and attitudes. Your presence in any circumstance adds to the energy of the situation. If you are in a state of worry and anxiety, you contribute tension. If you are in a state of Inner Peace, you contribute harmony. We are in control of our attitudes and we control what we contribute to any situation. We are in control of stopping ourselves from *reacting* to the world and instead learn how to *respond* to the world.

Next it is important that we take time to connect with our Inner Peace. Spending time with a sleeping infant reminds us that Inner Peace is our natural state of being. Inner Peace is our natural state of health. This can be done through quiet contemplation, meditation, walking in nature and putting ourselves in peaceful environments. Taking time to separate ourselves from the outer world and connecting with our inner world is vital to discovering our Inner Peace.

How do we change our state of being? We live in three phases of time: past, present and future. Release yourself from past regrets, guilt and resentments. It takes a tremendous amount of energy to live in the present while carrying around baggage from the past. There are many healers, therapists and self-help books that can guide you through various processes of clearing old and stale energy. If you take this first step, you will have less worry and anxiety to project into your future. As you become free of your fears, you will be able to imagine your future as fun-filled and joyous. You will have more "presence of mind" to manage the current stress that takes place on a daily basis. You will have more presence to change your *reactions* to *responses.*

Achieving Inner Peace does not mean that un-peaceful things stop happening. It's how you respond to them that allows you to live in a more peaceful state of being as you move through your day. You begin to radiate Inner Peace. Your responses to the tensions of the day uplift any situation. You will notice the difference, your family and friends will notice the difference, your coworkers will notice the difference and anyone you interact with during the day will be reminded of the Inner Peace that lies within them simply by observing your sense of peace and tranquility.

Will you reap the rewards of your work? You betcha!

Signs You Have Achieved Inner Peace

- The ability to enjoy living more fully and present in each moment.

- A tendency to think and act deliberately and spontaneously.

- A loss of interest in self judgment.

- A loss of interest in being involved with conflict.

- A loss of interest in judging and interpreting the actions of others.

- A loss of the ability to worry.

- Frequent, overwhelming episodes of appreciation.

- Feelings of connectedness with yourself, others and nature.

- Frequent bursts of "smiling through the heart".

- An increased susceptibility to kindness, generosity and the uncontrollable urge to extend it to others.

- An increasing tendency to allow things to unfold naturally, rather than resisting and manipulating them.

Life

Throughout the past week I have been given many opportunities to contemplate this event we call "life". It made me stop and realize just how many forms, meanings and expressions the word "life" encompasses on any given day.

In one week's time, I was called upon to attend a wake and help celebrate a life well lived; I was asked to send love for an individual slowly making their transition into death and was also asked to send hope for a woman undergoing cancer surgery. I've been asked to celebrate with a friend whose surgery made her body cancer free, and honor the 6th year anniversary of my partner killed in an automobile accident. I've celebrated the birthday of a great friend and officiated the marriage of a 78-year old couple that decided nine months of pre-marital classes required by their religion was too long to wait to enjoy the gift of being together. Ironically, nine months couldn't come soon enough for a young couple as I watched them at long last welcome their twin boys into the world. From birth to death, life came full circle for me this week.

Life is the space between birth and death. Most of us have approximately 80 years to experience the journey of life. I often refer to the word life as an acronym; whose corresponding letters mean **L**iving **I**n **F**ull **E**xpression. Some people experience life as unsettling and unsatisfying. Others experience life as the victim, the one always left out, short-changed, done wrong or faced with one tragedy after another. Still others experience life kicking and screaming, beating their chest like King-Kong, stealing energy from others and mistakenly thinking it will add more to their own. And some people experience life as marvelous and fascinating, full of great friends and excellent opportunities. What makes the difference?

Maybe it's karma. Maybe it's destiny. Maybe it's perception and choice. If we perceive life as a challenge, life will support us in bringing challenges we can handle. If we perceive life as an opportunity, life will support us in bringing experiences to enjoy. The same experiences perceived as a challenge for one present opportunity for another. We all have a choice in how we **perceive** life. We all have a choice in how we **invest** our life's energy. We all have a choice in how we **experience** life.

Life is a huge package ready for us to open, fully claim our greatness and call out that same greatness in others. Our perception makes all the difference--is it merely a "package" or a "gift"?

I am very blessed with a vocation, a "calling", to help others open their gift of life. I support others who have a deep desire to know their **presence**, feel their **power** and live their **passions**. Life is about living every day in full expression. How we choose to express ourselves determines whether life becomes a destination we dread or a journey to embrace.

Moving Beyond Doubts and Fears

It's Hell in the Hallway

Ever feel like you're standing in the middle of a long corridor of doors, all closed, and you're confused about what to do next? This often happens when you begin to consider making changes in your life. Doors may close before new ones open and you discover you're in the hallway and it feels like hell!

As you get conscious about your life, realizing there may be different possibilities available to you, a natural shift occurs in your energy. With this shift comes a renewed sense of creativity. Creativity brings new and exciting thoughts and ideas into your mind. As your mind contemplates these creative ideas, your attention shifts from what is--to what **can** be. As your attention shifts, so do your emotions, and you begin to wrap your feelings abound these new options. Your external world follows suit and things shift to match your internal thoughts and feelings. Life as you know it begins to change. With this shift, doors may close before new ones open and you discover you're in the hallway and it feels like hell!

You may suddenly become bored or restless, unable to concentrate on the tasks at hand. Sometimes if the change is long overdue, things may speed up rapidly. You may dream of a new job and suddenly find yourself downsized or transferred. You may consider making a move to a different state and have your landlord show up and give you notice unexpectedly. You may consider leaving a relationship that doesn't work anymore and your partner asks for a separation. Doors may close before new ones open and you discover you're in the hallway and it feels like hell!

So what do you do when you find yourself standing there with all doors closed?

First, recognize where you are and why you're there. You have begun to set things in motion with your internal shifts and the "ironic" events that are happening are the external changes necessary for you to move forward. Realize that the timing may be a little off for your comfort zone, but not for the larger picture. Remember, doors may close before new ones open and you'll discover you're in the hallway but now it doesn't feel quite as much like hell. Just keep breathing.

Next, maintain your focus on new possibilities. Hold the energy in thought and feeling for what you want to experience with the changes. It's OK to knock on a few doors and see if one opens to you. Maybe you will receive new insight or new information that can be helpful. Maybe you will be invited into a room to visit temporarily as you catch your breath before moving on. If you knock and hear someone say, "I hear you knocking but you can't come in," move on quickly and try another door--it's one sure sign that you're headed back to feeling like hell! Don't give up; breathe and embrace the new opportunities these open doors provide. It's okay to stand still and wait, cultivating patience.

As much as transition is welcomed, standing outside of your comfort zone never feels comfortable! Turn hell into heaven by celebrating the closing of the doors and affirming they are a sign that you are on your way to experiencing new openings and new beginnings.

Remember, the stairway to heaven begins with one-step-at-a-time.

Transforming Fear into Faith

FEAR is: **F**alse **E**vidence **A**ppearing **R**eal. In others words, most fear we experience is self manufactured – yep, we make it up! Think about it, most things you fear are things you *imagine* will or *may* happen to you in the future. This is your perception, but has little to do with the reality of the present moment. Your imagination is excellent at painting a very colorful, energy-catching picture of the fearful outcome you perceive. So vivid is this portrait that the fear appears real in your mind. Much of what you fear is based on something that happened in the past, to you or someone else, and you project the same fearful event happening to you in the future. Fear shows up in your life as worry, anxiety, restlessness, stress and tension.

Living in fear is like living your life in a dark, comfortable cave fearing the light outside. When you get too close to the edge, you project your fears into the light to keep you safe within the cave. The cave becomes your small circle of comfort, known as your "personal comfort zone." You know your existence to be what happens within this zone. As you move through your days, you do so with comfort and ease because you find trust and security in your cave. This "comfort zone" does not include all the things we fear. We leave those out of the equation, although the memories linger in our minds. Sometimes life extends an invitation to experience something new; to step outside your comfort zone. Or, maybe life in the cave becomes so boring you open the trunk of memories and try on a few to generate a little fear and wake you up a bit. Here is silly question: **"Why do you do this?!"** Because of fear! Even though it's **uncomfortable**, it is still within in your **"comfort zone,"** because fear is all you've known.

Franklin Roosevelt said, *"The only thing we have to fear is fear itself."* How can you begin to experience what life outside the cave is like? How can you stop your fear in order to step outside the comfort zone for a broader, richer life experience? How can you move from the darkness of the cave into the light of Truth? The answer is <u>faith</u>.

FAITH means: **F**ind **A**n **I**nfinite **T**ruth **H**ere. When you have faith, you are basing your life on Universal Principles or Infinite Truths, not on the *illusions* of your perceptions. What are the higher principles in which you believe? What is it **above all else** you know to be True? You may believe you are always connected to a Higher Power, or to God. You may believe an "inner wisdom" will direct you. You may believe all your prayers are heard and answered by this higher power. You may believe you are always being looked after and cared for. You may believe LOVE is greater than all your fears. Transforming your *fears* into *faith* is the key to living an abundantly rich, full and satisfying life. Faith means living your life with purpose.

Transforming your fear into faith requires you to:
> **Stop**: When you begin to feel fear
> **Acknowledge:** Your fear is making you feel alone, isolated and separated from love.
> **Remember Fear is**:
>> **F**alse **E**vidence **A**ppearing **R**eal
> **Tap into your faith**:
>> **F**ind **a**n **i**nfinite **t**ruth **h**ere
>
> Remember what you KNOW to be True

Allow your life's Infinite Truths transform your fear into faith. Step outside the comfort zone of your cave and walk into the light of Truth.

7 Sure Fire Ways to Sabotage Your Life:
A Witty Approach to Getting Back on Track if
You've Taken a Left Turn on the Road to Happiness

We all begin life traveling on the "road to happiness". At some point during this journey we may come to realize we turned left when we meant to turn right; which sidetracks us and puts us on plan "D" instead of plan "A". Life's not exactly "unhappy"; it's just not as fulfilling as we know it can be. We begin to feel as if life became "sabotaged" somewhere along the way. Now it's time to regain control and get back on track. You just need to readjust the road map!

That said, you are at "choice point." Maybe your choice is to continue what you're doing. OK. Just don't expect different results. Maybe your choice is to do something different to get different results. Once we set a direction in life, all our habits, behaviors, and choices either support or sabotage us in reaching that destination.

Let's take a look at some choices that may be sabotaging your life and solutions that will support getting you back on track.

#1 – Sabotage – Hit the floor running and don't stop 'til you drop. Fill your schedule to overflowing so that even taking a moment to catch your breath leaves you hyperventilating!

> **Solution** – Follow the airplane rule, "put your oxygen mask on first." Before you wake each morning, give yourself a moment to be still with yourself. Consciously take a few deep breaths. Visualize your day flowing smoothly and easily as you continue to consciously breathe. On today's calendar, block out 15 minutes and write your name in "pen". Set your cell phone

alarm. When the time arrives, use it to sit and do nothing but consciously breathe. Doing this ensures that you put on your oxygen mask first.

#2 – Sabotage – Hang out with toxic people who criticize, judge and carry around all their emotional baggage. For added effect and drama, make sure you unpack these people often.

Solution – Find the "balcony people" of your life. The people who always have "the best seats in the house"- those who make sure to see things "from the top." There is at least one person who sees the best in you. Make contact with them frequently. Let them cheer you on, inspire, motivate and support you. Begin to create your "team" of balcony people--your own cheering section! *(Keep in mind these people are different from the "nosebleed section people". They are the ones who can't see anything beyond the tips of their own noses and are committed to sabotaging anyone who attempts to get better seats than them.)*

#3 – Sabotage – Procrastinate! Why do today what you can put off until tomorrow!? Let's face it, if you let something go long enough, it may just disappear altogether and you'll be "off the hook," right?

Solution – Procrastination is a symptom of a deeper issue and instead of being "let off the hook," you're often left "hanging" your head in guilt. Why would you need to feel guilty? You don't, but you probably have a fear of succeeding and guilt guards you from this fear. (And those guards have some pretty hefty armor, don't they!?) Instead of lugging around all that heavy guilt, break free, connect with your "balcony people" and let them cheer you on to victory each and every time you follow through! Count all these victories and as they

60

add up, let them empower you to take the next step to success.

#4 – Sabotage – Hold onto the "right" attitude and make sure you're never wrong. It will keep you feeling like you're in control.
   Solution – It takes so much energy to be right all the time. Plus you really miss out on other ideas that can enhance your life. Learn to apologize. Learn to forgive. Learn to receive. Learn how to listen. *(I could be wrong, but my guess is that there will be many treasures waiting for you when you give yourself permission to not always be right!)*

#5 – Sabotage – Fill your life with clutter, stuff and mountains of paperwork. Keep all the drawers empty and the tabletops full!
   Solution – Clutter creates confusion. Confusion clogs your life's energy flow, your ability to think clearly and to be creative. Clear your space. Begin small. Sometimes it helps to set an alarm for 15 minutes and begin. Take in small bites. As you clear the clutter, even a small corner, allow yourself to feel good. Exhale. Let that good feeling motivate you for another 15 minutes. You'll be amazed at how quickly de-cluttering clears the mind.

#6 – Sabotage – Ignore self-care. After all, your mind and body are only the mechanics that keep your life running. You put gas in your car and send it for six month tune-ups; why is extending the mileage on a heap of metal and glass more important than extending the mileage on your life's journey?
   Solution – Taking care of the "self" is a #1 Priority! It is important to remember all areas of self: mind, body and spirit. To begin, make one change in one area.

For the body: eat a piece of fruit every day, drink a glass of water, and say one nice thing about yourself when you look in the mirror. For the mind: have an intellectually stimulating conversation with someone; read a book; watch a group of children discovering the world at a playground during your lunch break. For the spirit: sit quietly every day, subscribe to a daily inspiration, and share your gratitude daily. You'll be amazed at how much more mileage you get with just a little self care.

#7 – Sabotage – Expect perfection or "black and white" solutions for everything. If it's perfect, there's no room for option or choice, which means you don't have to deal with it!

Solution - There is no such thing as "perfect." Perfect is a relative term. Striving to be perfect fits into the category of needing to be right. Redefine your standards. Consider the option of making gray the "new black" when it comes to savvy thinking!

In reality, each of us practice all 7 of these sabotaging behaviors, so you're not alone. But you're also not necessarily in the best of company, either. These alternate ways of thinking and problem solving solutions allow you to begin to make a shift in the way you live your life, make the right turn and get back on track.

Choose one solution and begin to put it into practice. You can make a change to empower yourself; and you can ask for help in creating a new pattern. Be inspired this week to stop sabotaging your life and get back on the road to happiness.

Managing "What If"

"What if" are two of the most powerful words in our language. "What if" is the key that unlocks our imagination. Our imagination opens the door to the world of possibilities. Sounds wonder-filled doesn't it? We have the power to change our lives with the "what if" key.

It is vitally important that we learn to manage "what if." Without conscious management, we use the "what if" key to open our default programming. The default programming was installed in us as children by parents, family, and community that were not very awake or enlightened. Through no fault of their own, they did their best in programming us on how to experience life. Now, at this level of our spiritual evolution, we know a better way.

We know that our thoughts, our imagination and our beliefs are reflected in our physical and emotional energy field. And that energy field sends out signals, similar to radio signals. Our signals "tune" us into similar frequencies. We attract people, places and situations that are on the same wavelength as we are.

We get into uncomfortable moods which happen daily. Without new management skills, we begin to "what if" ourselves into a worried and anxious state. It goes something like this: First we have a situation presented to us by life that makes us feel uncomfortable in some way. We begin thinking about this situation. The "what if" game begins to play out in our mind. Mental images of the "what if" begin to form. The images become worse and worse. Feelings are evoked from what our imagination has created. All our senses become engaged in fear and we literally have to shut down in an exhausted state of mind. Unconsciously we have used the "what if" key to open the default programming. We have used our mind to imagine the possibilities that bring us the most fear.

Take a moment to walk though this process in relationship to something that made you uncomfortable this week. Perhaps something about finances or a relationship challenge or maybe something happened at your job. Where did your mind go? Did you fall into worry and anxiety? Did you care for yourself or scare yourself?

When we learn to manage the "what if", a buzzer sounds each time the default programming is about to take over. We become empowered to redirect our imagination. We stop the runaway train of thinking from taking us downhill and redirect it upwards to new and hopeful possibilities. The process is the same but the pattern of thinking changes. The difference is we use our thoughts to bring us joy rather than pain. Instead of the images becoming worse and worse, they become brighter and better.

The best way to learn how to manage "what if" is to practice. You can practice by setting time aside daily to imagine, to "what if". Moving through your day becomes positive and joy-filled. With daily practice, two things happen. One, you become proficient in managing the "what if" and two, you tune your radio signals to a higher frequency. Through practicing the positive use of your "what if" key, your life begins to unfold in new and exciting ways.

I invite you to share your experiences with me as you learn to manage your "what if".

Let it Be Easy

What's your reaction to these four words? Do you push against them while grumbling something like "yea right!" or do you sigh, releasing the breath you've been holding in for the past three minutes because you are frustrated with the day? Were you taught that anything worth having is worth working for and the harder the work, the more valuable the prize? The good news is that you don't have to buy into this belief any longer! You can let your life be easy and even more rewarding than ever before.

The great part about setting a new pace for your life is that it *can* be easy, no hard work required. By accepting this affirmation into your day you release all that you held onto and let yourself "go with the flow". You can begin to enjoy the Divine flow of the Universe, the perfect flow of life. The challenge comes in the acceptance that life *can* be easy, rewarding and full of fun and joy. Are you ready to change the beliefs you were taught and accept a natural flow of life?

The Divine paradox is that when you let go and stop *trying* to make a rewarding life, that is exactly what you get, a rewarding life! When you "Let it Be Easy" the joy you feel, the gifts you get, and the valuable prizes you receive are far greater than anything you could accomplish through your efforts of trying. And that's where the challenge is, in the "letting go." However, it can be more challenging than you think! Take a moment to consider if you are ready and willing to let go of your old beliefs that either caused you to feel exhausted in your efforts or depressed because you didn't get the prize you wanted. Are you willing to invest your energy and effort in creating a new habit? Are you ready to "Let it Be Easy?"

Here are steps that can support you in creating an easy life!

1. Observe – Become the observer of your life.

Pay attention to your inner dialogue. What kind of conversations do you have with yourself? What kinds of conversations are you having with others? What do you talk about, complain about? Observe when you feel frustrated, tired, anxious, or worried. When you learn to be the witness of your life, you may be surprised at what you will discover. Observe without judgment.

2. Stop – The first rule when you find that you are digging yourself into a hole is to "stop digging." Some people find it helpful to mentally say the word "stop" as they begin to create new habits. Remember to do this without judgment, because when you judge yourself you have begun reinforcing the old habit again.

3. Know – Know there is a different way for you to experience life. Know that you were born to live in a Divine flow of life's energy that is filled with fun and joy. You were born to live a life that brings out the best in you and has a place for you to share your gifts and talents for the greater good of all. If this is a stretch for your belief system, imagine the kind of life you would create and the feelings you would have if you won the lottery or inherited a grand amount of money. How would you create your life differently? This image will help you realize that you do know, and that you have this knowing wrapped in a prison that you believe will only come true when something magical happens. Knowing frees your dream life from prison.

4. Breathe – When you are frustrated or challenged you hold your breath or take shallow breaths. By learning how to take deep breaths, both inhaling and exhaling fully, several thing happen. One, you affirm that you are alive! Life is breath and without breath, there is no life. Second, you affirm you are willing to receive all that life has to offer as well as give freely. Simply by learning to breathe fully, you are letting go, you are living more balanced and you are putting yourself in the Divine flow.

5. Affirm – Affirm, "Let it Be Easy." Make this a daily affirmation. By affirming what you want, "Easy," and how you want your life to flow, "Let it Be," you are reprogramming your belief system. In order to stop an old habit you have to learn to create a new one. Redirect your thoughts toward creating a new habit by affirming what you want.

You can go through these five steps several times a day. When you are frustrated looking for your keys, an important paper, or running late for an appointment, affirm "Let it Be Easy." You will begin to observe something exciting happening to your life. Things that were hard will now be easy. The joy of life that is already in you will begin to be palpable. You will begin to see and feel the changes happening within you and reflect without. You will witness that you feel lighter, more relaxed. And you will attract new conversations into your life, along with new invitations to experience fun coming your way. Embrace it! You will witness a miracle happening! Let it Be Easy.

Trust Your Gut

Life is energy in motion. We are constantly aware and "reading" the energy of the world around us. Each one of us has an internal guidance system. Similar to the GPS in transportation, it reads the energy around us and feeds back directions through our intuition. This is true for everyone. Some people are more in tune and trust their intuition more than others.

When I ask audiences to place their hand on their gut, typically they place their hand on their abdomen, the area around the belly button. Consider that your bellybutton marks the place where the umbilical cord connected you to your mother. This connection was the source of nourishment as you were a developing embryo. Your intuition, your "gut instinct", is the source of nourishment as you develop your relationship with the world. Intuition can be more of a "knowing" rather than a "feeling".

More important than how you receive and communicate with your intuitive guidance system is the question, "How do you respond to it?" Do you trust your gut? Trust is the key word. Do you **trust** the information you receive from the source that nourishes you? When you trust your gut and follow its guidance, you will always be aligned with your core self, your Divine Self.

Think back to the last time you had a knowing about something, an action you could take or a choice you could make. Did you trust your gut or did you ask several people what "they thought you should do?" Were you surprised to discover they told you exactly what you already knew? Or did you discover that no one else's opinion felt as strong as your gut feeling? Perhaps you went with someone else's idea and found that you were not satisfied with the results and you ended up regretting that you followed someone else's advice.

Or maybe you moved into your left brain and began processing the guidance. When you find yourself considering options, making the list of good and bad on a sheet of paper, thinking and rethinking the action over and over again, you are intellectualizing your choice. Realize that you have <u>left your gut and gone to your head.</u> You have stopped "feeling" what to do and have begun to "process" what to do.

When you learn to trust your gut, you realize that you have an internal source that will guide, direct and nourish you. Building trust with your intuition is much like building trust with a best friend. It takes conscious effort to keep communications open, to listen and to ask for assistance. Sometimes your guidance doesn't make sense to you or your family or friends. Sometimes it doesn't even make sense to your logical thinking. It is very important that you learn to trust your gut. The idea that Eckhart Tolle presents in his book "*A New Earth: Awakening to your Life's Purpose*" is that when you "awaken" you know your True identity; you experience living your life from the inside out. In order to live an awakened life, you need to develop an intimate relationship with your intuition, and trust its guidance.

You Have Arrived!

You catch a thought, an inspiration pops into your mind. A light bulb goes off. You begin to toss it around in your head, giving it consideration. Your mind begins to wrap around the possibilities as you sit with it for a few days in contemplation. Your emotions begin to engage in this now fabulous idea. It flows from your mind down into your heart and takes on a life of its own. Each pulsating heartbeat creates a new impulse of energy, a spark that ignites a passion inside you. Your heart envisions the idea as a real possibility for your life. You become aligned with the idea: heart, mind and emotions. Your inner voice exclaims *"Wow, I can do that!"*, proclaims *"I believe this is possible!"*, and confirms *"What an absolutely fabulous idea!"*

Your silent words, your thoughts, your emotions, your passion become a prayer. But they don't go unnoticed. There's another force listening. The Universe hears you! It begins to get all the players in place. There is a shift in the energy of the Universe. Heaven and earth are moved for you. People are directed toward you, as if you are a magnetic field. The red carpet is rolled out. The door of opportunity is put in your line of sight. The runway is lined with everything you need: information, people, places, resources. Everything you need is ready, in place and waiting for you! The Universe prepares to welcome a new magnificence into the world!

You stand on the red carpet, captivated by all that surrounds you. Chills of exhilaration run through your body as the hair on your arms stand on end with the energy of excitement. You KNOW in your heart this is it! This is the dream you've waited for, and you are ready! The Universe celebrates your arrival. Fireworks explode above you. You begin to walk down the red carpet toward the door of a new self. You are amazed at the people who suddenly appear out of nowhere to serve as your guides. Crowds form along the runway and people you don't recognize smile and pat you on the back as you walk past them. They cheer and congratulate you. You are in total awe of the words of inspiration whispered in your ear. All the puzzle pieces have fallen easily into place and you watch in utter amazement! Finally! You arrive at the door.

You know that on the other side of that door is the manifestation of your dream. It is the dynamic idea come to fruition. It is the passion of your heart, the ideal job of a lifetime, the partner of your dreams, and it is abundance beyond measure. It is a calling you have heard in your most silent moments; a calling that has taken years to be heard outside of your own mind.

It is your magnificent Self!

With your hand on the doorknob, you slowly begin to turn the handle, feeling it move as your heart skips a beat. The pulsing in your head has become louder. There is no more waiting. No hesitation. You are ready! **YES!** The time is **Now**! **Now**! **Now**! …. Then, you freeze. Everything stops. The roaring crowds who cheered you are now replaced with an all too familiar deafening silence within your mind.

The clouds of doubt surround you. *"I don't know"* arrives. It covers the vision of your heart with a veil of self doubt and confusion. Your deepest fears of unworthiness flood you. You feel as if you're drowning.

"What if I'm making this all up? What if I open this door and nothing's there?"

You hear the word **"NO"** screamed on the loud speaker, *"NO, don't touch! NO, that's not for you! NO, don't bother me! NO, you're not good enough! NO, you can't have that! NO, not this time, NO, not now! You thought all this was for you? You've got to be kidding! Why would you be worthy of such enlightenment?"*

The fear of abandonment and disapproval dims the energy that once burned so bright within you. You melt into a puddle of self doubt. Your knees lock, your legs begin to shake. You are frozen with fear. A hush falls over the crowd, followed by silence.

You stand with your hand on the door of your Magnificent Self...paralyzed.

Putting Into
Practice

Your Magnificent Self

Who do you know that reflects a "Magnificent Self?" We all know someone. Oprah is a prime example of someone who embraces her Magnificent Self. She uses her passions and multitude of resources to motivate and inspire others. She shines her light brightly into places of darkness to wake-up the world, call together other bright lights and beckon us all into oneness.

It is important to know that we each have a Magnificent Self waiting to be expressed and shared with the world. It is a Self that comes from within. You can't stand in the bright light of another Magnificent Self and become Magnificent, it doesn't work that way.

People of Magnificence ask you to cultivate and develop the qualities of greatness within so that you can become your own Magnificent Self! Where do you begin?

Here are just a few qualities that define a Magnificent Self:

1. Take 100% Responsibility for Yourself and Your Actions
You are 100% responsible for your perceptions, reactions and your responses to life. You are 100% responsible for how you experience the events of your life. When you are willing to take full responsibility for life, you no longer blame or accuse others for things not working in your life.
You are empowered to make apologies, clear up misspoken conversations and make amends quickly. You commit your energy to bringing life together in a healthy, loving flow.

2. Live in the Spirit of Abundance
Being in the flow of abundance is key to knowing there is always enough. "Enough" is measured in terms of ideas,

creativity, time, money, opportunities, and of course love. Letting go of a belief in "lack" or "not enough" is paramount to being a Magnificent Self. It also supports you in letting go of having the desire to compete or have more. As you claim your plenty, you are able to take all you need and give back more knowing there is always enough.

3. Gratitude is a Magic Key
Living with an "attitude of gratitude" gives you an open perspective of life. Gratitude keeps the energy of life flowing. Gratitude is the key that helps you breathe in life more fully and allow its experiences to expand both your inner self and your vision of possibilities.

4. Know the Divine Paradox of Life
Understanding this concept plays a tremendous role in how you navigate life's speed bumps. Situations that appear to "get in your way" are the very experiences you need to "overcome" in order to get where you are going.

The journey to expressing your Magnificent Self happens **one-step-at-a-time.** When you become sidetracked, discouraged or stuck and begin to spin your wheels, step back and be 100% responsible for your perception. As you change the energy of the little things that "get in your way," you are actually taking the next step forward.

5. Live by a Higher Wisdom
Living by a higher wisdom lets you know you are an intricate part of life's complex puzzle. When you connect to your higher wisdom, you are linked to your Magnificent Self. Living in this consciousness supports you in thinking "outside the box" and in creating habits that **supports** life, not take it away.

6. Your Life is Your Message

Knowing that entire your life's purpose is to deliver a message, you are committed to giving your Magnificent Self back to the world as a gift. Your life has a higher purpose and meaning. You are authentic. You walk your talk. You practice what you preach and you know you are making a difference in the world; shining your light on others so they too have the opportunity to experience living as their Magnificent Self!

Take a moment and remember, you cannot be an audience member to become your magnificent self. Being on Oprah or simply listening to her messages isn't the answer. Thinking like Oprah is.

You must be a participant in your own life's story, deliver your own messages and generate your own light. Only then can you truly reflect your Magnificent Self.

What's in a Word?

Words impact our lives and have more power than we can imagine. Words create the core of our communication, personal expression and are powerful enough to manipulate our reality and existence. Think I'm speaking "out of context?" Then, why at age 50 are you still allowing the critical words spoken to you by an angry parent at age 10 to control your life today?

Words create an image or perception of ourselves or what we believe others perceive us to be and have an energy that either increases or diminishes our self worth and confidence. Words are power, and yet we are often careless with what we allow to roll off our tongues during everyday conversation. How many of us really *"think before we speak"*?

Here's an example. Right now, "try" to stop reading this message. You either stopped reading or you continued to read, but you did not "try" to stop reading. Webster's definition of the word "try" reads, *"to make an attempt."* The word "try" keeps us in process rather than takes us to completion. Yet most of us habitually make daily use of the word "try." "Try" is a word that tears us down because it traps our energy in process mode rather than free our energy in expressive mode. When you say, *"I am "trying" to accomplish something,"* you are really saying, *"I am making an attempt but not really doing it."* If you say, *"I am trying to change a bad habit,"* you are really saying *"I am making an attempt but getting nowhere."*

Here's another example. The word "decision" means, *"to cut, as if with a knife."* Its root is related to the words suicide, insecticide, pesticide, and homicide. All words related to death. It's no wonder we often feel stuck when we are in the position of making a "decision."

81

Unconsciously we are saying: *"If I take one option the other option will die. What if my decision is a mistake and there's no turning back?"* By replacing the word "try" with the word "choice," we change the power of our options. The word "choice" means, *"making a selection, the opportunity* or power of choosing" to live in the power of choice frees and expands our energy. The word choice builds up life creates options.

Just think how much we drain our precious life's energy when we say, *"I am "trying" to make a "decision!"* We become exhausted, frustrated and often times give up all together. I say, *"stop trying!"* and never make another "decision" in your life! Use the **power** of your words to **affirm** the choices you claim for your life.

Here are a few other words worth rethinking:

When you say "but" you negate all the words preceding it.
("I like you but…")

The word "just" minimizes the words following.
("I just want to say …")

The word "remember" affirms, the words "don't forget" assign judgment.
("Remember to pick me up after school")

What's in a word? The energy of your life! Empower yourself to change your life by changing your vocabulary! Think about it!

Self Care On the Run

Self-care may be important but I'm guessing it gets put on the bottom of your "to do" list. Who has time for self-care while working fulltime, managing a household, car pooling the kids and participating in their many activities? Not to mention the time and effort needed keep the fire burning in your significant relationship?!

There is one simple answer: Breathing. It's more of a survival tool than you think.

I know you already breathe; however, the breathing I'm talking about is **conscious breathing**. Conscious breathing is when you place your attention on breathing **while** you're breathing. It is interesting that when you pay attention to breathing while actually breathing, your breath automatically becomes slower and deeper. Try it right now. Take three deep breaths, inhaling deeply, and exhaling fully. Go on, try it.

Do you feel more relaxed? Did you exhale more on your last breath than you did on the first? Did your thoughts slow down? Did you become more present in the moment? These are just a few of the benefits of conscious breathing.

Conscious breathing is an excellent way to care for yourself while on the run. Most people's normal breathing pattern is shallow and uses a very small upper portion of the lung's capacity. When you are feeling anxious, your breath can become quick and shallow; your body goes into "fight-or-flight" response.

You may even catch yourself holding your breath in tense moments. When you don't exhale fully you build up carbon monoxide in your lungs which acts as an anesthetic and can actually make you more lethargic and tired. When you consciously breathe, take notice how your lungs expand and how much oxygen you take in. Your breathing is a reflection of the pace of your energy.

Your body has a physiological response to your breath. You can slow down your racing mind by slowing down your breath. Chemicals in your brain become more balanced, the level of oxygen in your cells rises and your pulse rate slows down; all of which are a direct result of your breathing. Your body will welcome the oxygen and reward you with clearer thinking. The cells of your body will get the food they need to reproduce healthy cells. You will be better prepared to handle stress when it happens. The benefits of conscious breathing for your body, mind, and Spirit are endless. Conscious breathing is the ultimate in self-care.

Begin a new regiment of self-care by creating the habit of consciously breathing into your day. Conscious breathing can be done anywhere, anytime and can easily fit into your busy schedule. The next time you're sitting at a traffic light, take a few conscious breaths. While you're waiting for the children to get out of school, consciously breathe. When you hit the start button on the microwave, stand there for a few minutes and consciously breathe. Consciously breathe while you're in the shower. Discover what works for you. Celebrate your ability to practice self-care by setting a new pace for your busy life with conscious breathing. Your body, mind and Spirit will enjoy the benefits!

Raising Your Self-Esteem

Esteem is the value and worth we place on something. Having a healthy self-esteem places value and worth on you as a human being. Low self-esteem prevents you from claiming your "good" in life, and sharing your unique gifts and talents with the world. A healthy self-esteem raises your Spiritual Self-Esteem. Developing a Spiritual Self-Esteem will lead the way for you to discover and live your life's purpose. We can make a radical change in our self-esteem by moderating and changing our inner dialogue. Critical self-talk plays a major role in how much we value or under-value ourselves.

Here are some choices you can make to help develop a healthy self-esteem.

1. Stop Comparing

When you compare yourself to others, you create the energy of competition. Each one of us is unique with great gifts to share. If your self-esteem is low you may have the tendency to maximize the good qualities in others which then magnifies your weaknesses.

2. Accept Compliments

When someone offers you a compliment, "Thank you" is the perfect response. A response that qualifies or justifies the compliment is a way of devaluing yourself.

3. Ask for Verification

If someone doesn't return your call, check the facts instead of making assumptions. Critical self-talk assumes the worst. Stop making up stories and ask "Why?" or "Is there a problem?" Most times another's reaction has nothing to do with you.

4. Stop Shielding Yourself

Change the "I should" to "I choose to/or I choose not to". When you get caught up in the "shoulda, woulda, coulda and I must" syndrome, you make unrealistic demands on yourself that may stop you from ever being good enough.

5. Don't Label Behaviors

When you do something stupid, say, "I did something stupid" rather than labeling your self by your behavior by saying that you are stupid. This will help you to be more confident as well as stop labeling others and comparing.

Placing a small value on yourself doesn't serve anyone; and you are here for a purpose that will help you life large. Begin to live large by changing the way you value yourself. Consider these daily steps to raise your self-esteem to a healthy level and take your place in the circle of life! You're worth it!

Ask For What You Want

How many times have you wanted something but were afraid to ask? I recently heard someone mention that they are accustomed to getting what they wanted because they have no problem asking for it. Their belief is that if there is a 50% chance they will get a "yes" answer, then why not? Many of us believe the opposite. If there is a 50% chance of getting a "no" answer, then why bother?

In the recent books, movies and CD's about the Universal Law of Attraction ("The Secret" and "The Art of Allowing" to name just a few) you have learned that knowing what you want and asking for what you want are the ways you tap into the Universal flow of abundance. Asking for what you want is the way you put your order into the ethers. It is the way you declare what you are ready and willing to receive.

There is a great teaching that says, "ask and it is given" or "ask and ye shall receive". Yet, most of us stand in our own fear, afraid to ask. We have feelings of unworthiness. Our default programming, that is filled with viruses by the way, tells us that we are not worthy to be given whatever it is we want. We make the answer to our question, "no", before we even ask. Soon we stop asking.

When I was growing up and I asked my mom for something I wanted, her typical response would be, "and people in hell want ice water". Of course this set up the default programming. I was programmed to think that when you ask, you will be rejected. The message was, you can't always have what you want and you will always live unsatisfied. This leads to thinking and feeling that your life is hell. As I developed new perspectives of life and became more empowered with the ways life can be experienced, I quickly quarantined that virus.

Our emotions are energy in motion. Our emotions charge our thoughts, putting them into motion. Our thoughts create our belief system and our belief system creates the energy field that acts like a magnet attracting those people and situations into our lives that resonate with our energy.

Look around you. Do you attract people and situations that are a part of the bigger picture of what you say you want out of life? Is there someone who may have information for you? Is there someone who may hold the key that will open doors for you? Is there a situation that is your golden opportunity? Is there someone standing right there in front of you, a representative of the Universal flow, and you are afraid to ask for what you want?

Here is your opportunity for the week. Stop letting your default programming and your fear of rejection stop you. If there is something you want, ask for it. Begin with the person or situation right in front of you. ASK FOR WHAT YOU WANT!

Learning to Receive

Many of us were raised with the teaching "it is better to give than to receive". This teaching, which was intended to make us feel kind and good, did just the opposite! We learned how to drain ourselves with no clue how to refill. It taught us there is only so much to go around and we shouldn't be selfish, so we never really learned to receive. This set up a pattern of imbalance and a created a generation of people that felt deprived and depressed.

Energetically drained with a desire to return to balance and feel rich and happy, we reacted by becoming over-consumers. We filled ourselves from the "outside", attempting to be satisfied on the "inside". We filled our houses, basements, attics and closets with more stuff than we could ever possibly use. We overfilled our bodies with food that we could never digest. We built an empire based on credit; spending what we did not have, because we never learned to receive.

A new teaching has emerged, showing us there is an Infinite and Divine flow of energy in the Universe. When we live in that flow, we feel satisfied on the inside while enjoying the pleasures of life on the outside. In order for us to be in that flow, we need to learn to receive.

When I first learned of this teaching, I had to put forth extra effort in regaining my balance and getting into the flow. One of the ways I did this was to remember each day offered me many gifts. I had to train myself to stay awake and receive whatever gifts were brought into my life that day. I found a terra-cotta angel kneeling and holding a gift in her hands. I painted the gift gold and placed the statue on a shelf by the front door. Every time I left the house, I would look at the angel and remind myself to receive all the gifts this day had to offer. As I walked through my day I was amazed at the many gifts that were given to me. It was pleasantly overwhelming!

I used this affirmation: "I am open and receptive to the gifts of this day." I paid attention to my body language, keeping my palms open, my shoulders back and head up, all signs of receptivity. I counted how many times I could say "thank-you" in a day, knowing each one represented a gift I received. I learned how to practice self-care and fill myself up from the inside.

There is a balance in giving and receiving and an endless abundance of life's energy. I began to see myself as a vessel, filling to an overflowing capacity. Because I learned to receive, I discovered I was better able to give generously while remaining full and in the Divine flow. And in receiving, I feel good and kind and full of joy.

Discover what gifts are waiting for **you** today and be sure to receive them with an open heart and mind.

Getting Unstuck

You will never get unstuck by focusing on how stuck you feel. When you are overwhelmed with thoughts and feelings of being stuck, your creative energies shut down and taking action can feel impossible. Focusing on how stuck you feel will create more situations that make you feel stuck. Stuck can go from bad to worse quickly.

There is hope. There is a tool that you have available to you right now. It is the key for shifting your focus and redirecting your feelings. It is one of the most valuable tools you have access to that can free you and move you forward.

The tool is **GRATITUDE**. Making use of this tool can release your thoughts, elevate your feelings and get you unstuck.

As Einstein said, "You cannot solve the problem at the level of the problem." So focusing on being stuck will never free you. But when you are willing to direct some energy, even a little bit of energy, towards that for which you are grateful, you will take your focus off the problem and open the doors to the creative flow. Gratitude keeps you in the flow of life, the flow of creativity.

Begin small, if that is all you can do as a first step. Right where you are, look around and list a few things you are grateful for. Read over the items slowly; fully experience the feeling of gratitude. Allow this energy to flow through you, opening your heart, softening your mind. You know that you cannot be in anxiety, worry or fear when you are in gratitude. That is why this tool is so powerful. Gratitude opens your mind and your heart. You cannot be grateful and judge at the same time. You may have to take baby steps for a few days until you begin to feel the energy of being stuck moving.

When you are ready, you can take the next step. Write a letter of gratitude. Your letter can be written to the Universe, God, Spirit, even yourself, in your personal journal. You may want to think of a situation that you are really not happy about and feeling stuck in. Think of yourself on the other side of this problem, living in the solution. Begin to write how grateful you are about the outcome you are experiencing. Engage your senses. What do you see? Who is in the picture? What are you doing? How are you feeling? What are you experiencing? Really get into the letter as much as possible. You are also engaging your imagination, creating a visual, opening to the creative flow.

Read this letter at least once a day. Schedule time to sit and read your letter, then close your eyes and allow yourself to see and feel the vision your letter creates. Pay attention to how "in the flow" you feel. Feel the energy of life begin to move through you. You may need a few days, or perhaps weeks to go through this process depending on how stuck you felt. Be patient with yourself. I assure you, using the tool of gratitude will move you from stuck to flowing.

Expanding Your Practice

Stop the Leaks and Reframe

Here is a great technique I have been using in my coaching practice. I call it "Stop the Leaks and Reframe".

Have you ever found yourself obsessing about a situation that doesn't seem to be working for you? It could be an unbalanced relationship; a frustrating situation at work with your boss, co-worker or company policies that just don't make sense. Or, maybe you're depressed with your body size, shape or overall health. Whatever the case, you find yourself entangled in the situations of life. Your "energy well" has become depleted. You feel, drained, off balance and unable to find your center.

The first step in the solution is to "Stop the Leaks!"
The top three energy leaks are caused by:
1. Perception
2. Obsessing
3. Stressing

When you live in a state of stress and frustration, you are like a container with holes in it. When you are constantly thinking about your problems, all the energy you pour into this container to move throughout your day leaks out. As a result, you become drained, exhausted and frustrated. Stressful living then becomes a self fulfilling prophecy.

The first step in stopping the leaks is to get honest and take an assessment of the situation. I always call on "The Serenity Prayer" for guidance.

"God, Grant me the serenity to accept the things I cannot change, courage to change the things I can, and the wisdom to know the difference."

First, name the things you cannot change in the situation. You cannot change other people's way of thinking, feeling or behaving. You cannot change the way others express themselves in the world. **Stop trying!** There are predetermined situations in your life you can do nothing about. **Accept them**. Without acceptance, you will not stop the leaks. Until you stop leaking your energy into things you cannot change, you will always be un-empowered in life.

As you take time to assess stressful situations, ask for the wisdom to be discerning in the things you cannot change. Ask for the courage to change the things you can change (perception, obsession, etc.) Move into the mindset of acceptance.

The second step in the solution is to "reframe." Now that you've stopped the leaks and are at a place of acceptance, you are ready to reframe. Reframing is about recreating the scenario in your mind to one that works for you. One that brings you peace and makes you feel okay. In other words, you have the power within your mind to tell the story in a way that makes you feel good about yourself.

In an unbalanced relationship, stop expecting someone else to make you feel a certain way. Accept and take responsibility for the way you feel and how you process and express your feelings. Then, reframe the relationship in your mind into one that you express your love and respect to your partner. You become the one who feels loving. Living and acting from this place of love changes the dynamics of the relationship.

If you are frustrated about a situation at work, stop blaming, projecting and attacking others. Stop the leaks.

Reframe the position you have at your job into one that brings you peace. As you work day by day with this attitude of peace and empowerment, you will be amazed how work seems to change around you.

Apply these same concepts to body issues. Stop being angry and critical about your body. Begin to reframe your relationship with your body into one that is more loving, peaceful and accepting. Your body will respond with more energy and strength.

I challenge you this week to change a situation in your life by using this process. Experience how fulfilling and overflowing with abundance your life can truly become when you "Stop the Leaks and Reframe."

The Ultimate Intelligence - Spiritual

The Holistic Community is built around the belief in the trinity of mind, emotions and spirit being the foundation for a wholesome life. And now scholars agree. In the earlier part of the twentieth century the term IQ, (Intelligent Quotient) became the measurement of rational intelligence or "what we think".

A decade ago, Daniel Goleman popularized EQ, the measurement of Emotional Intelligence, or "what we feel". And now, more recently scholar and author Dana Zohan, and her husband Ian Marshall, bring us "SQ/Spiritual Intelligence" or "what we are". An awareness of each level of intelligence raises the effectiveness of the others.

Zohar and Marshall bring the Eastern and Western traditions together using the symbol of the lotus. The outer petals represent Intelligence, the middle layer the emotions and the center represents the spiritual self. As we look at the lotus symbol we first see the outer petals. We become aware of "what we think" on the outer surfaces of life. As we move inward to the middle layer our thinking is more effective when we know "what we feel". And as we bring our thinking and feeling together we move inward to the center of the lotus and become more effective when we know "what we are".

This is very exciting! Not necessarily the idea of "measuring" but the acknowledgement of the three "Q's" creating the trinity of Mind, Emotion and Spirit. And in the Holistic Health field, we understand that when we are connected to the Spirit of ourselves first and foremost and get connected to "what we are" at the core of our being, we are better able to get clearer about "what we feel". And as we tap into the higher vibration feelings of love, joy, and peace, the emotions that create, and support life, we align ourselves with our highest intelligence. This intelligence, "what we think" is our inner genius. It is a wisdom that clearly guides us in making choices, and taking action for the highest and best for all.

Here is how Danah Zohar defines SQ, "I think Spirituality is located in the deep self, which is ultimately connected to the ground of reality itself. Physicist would call this the quantum vacuum. Religious people would call it God. Buddhist would call it the soulful being. Doesn't matter what you call it. Even in physics there is a kind of fundamental reality as the base of things. Spiritual Intelligence is described as "the intelligence with which we address and solve problems of meaning and value, the intelligence with which we can place our actions and our lives in a wider, rich, meaning-giving context, the intelligence with which we can assess the one course of action or one-path is more meaningful than another."

In their book "Connecting With Our Spiritual Intelligence," 12 transformative principles of Spiritual Intelligence are identified.

1. **Self-awareness -** To know what I believe in, value and what deeply motivates me.

2. **Vision and Value-led** – Acting from principles, deep beliefs and living accordingly.

3. **Positive Use of Adversity** – Ability to learn from mistakes, grow and learn from setbacks and suffering.

4. **Holistic**– Ability to see larger patterns, relationships, connections. Sense of belonging.

5. Compassion – Quality of 'feeling-with" and deep empathy.

6. Celebration of Diversity – Regarding other people for their differences, not despite them.

7. Field-Independent – To be able to stand against the crowd and hold your own convictions.

8. Ask Fundamental "Why" Questions – Need to understand things, to get to the bottom of them.

9.Ability to Reframe – Stand back from situation/problem and see the bigger picture; see problems in wider context.

10. Spontaneity - To live in and respond to the moment.

11. Sense of Vocation – To feel called upon to serve, to give something back.

12. Humility – Sense of being a player in the larger drama and true place in the world.

How do you raise your SQ? By taking the first step, raise your Self-Awareness.

Use Your Insight to Improve Your Eyesight

When you develop your insight, the world you see through your eyesight changes. Many of us were taught to see the world around us in an objective rather than a reflective way. We were taught to evaluate and react to it rather than observe it. Your insight is the sight you have from within--your intuition. Each one of us is intuitive.

You have the ability to develop your insight and change the way you see the world before you with your eyesight. Insight is defined as "seeing intuitively; the power of observation". Learning to use your insight, your inner knowing, to observe the world in front of your eyes shifts your perspective. It gives you a broader view of life, allowing your interactions and the choices you make to be the highest and best for all concerned.

We all have insight and intuition. We were never taught how to tap into it, how to communicate with it or how to use it as we navigate life. It takes concentrated practice to trust your insight, to know the language, the inner knowing, until it becomes the first response. Each of us has an inner language that our intuition uses to communicate and that language is unique to us. The messages, the feelings, the voice or the vision and the interpretation will be different for each of us. Learning to tune in to your insight takes daily practice. The clearer the communication you have with your intuition, the better your focus will be.

How do you tune-in and develop your insight? Create a daily time of quiet. Sit and focus on your breathing. It can be helpful to you and your mind chatter to say to yourself, "breathe in, and breathe out." Do this for a few moments until you can feel your body relaxing. Think of a situation you want to know more about, perhaps a situation at work or with your family. Bring the thoughts about the situation to your mind. You may be able to see it as an inner picture or just a thought. Imagine yourself looking down at the situation as if you were above it. Make the statement: "I want some insight about this situation." Then, listen silently for a few moments, visualize what you see and really become aware of the thoughts you begin thinking. Quietly pay attention. You may want to have a pad and pencil ready before you begin to take notes or jot some points.

Don't be frustrated if it doesn't "come to you" right away, especially if this is the first time you tuned-in. It may take a few attempts until you trust that you will get insight and then be able to relax and view with trust. Trust enough to relax and step outside your own perception of the situation that may be blocking your higher vision. Depending on the situation, you may want to ask some questions during this "tuning in" time. "What can I do for the highest good of all?" Wait for an answer. "What can I learn from this situation?" "Is there anything else I need to know right now?" Jot down what comes to your mind. It may not make sense at first, however as the day passes, the messages will become more clear to you. Consistency is key. The more you tap into your intuitive self, the more in focus your life will become. Make the time. It is time well invested.

See if you are able to hold a new perception for your eyesight. What are you seeing in the situation based on what you learned from your tuning-in session? Perhaps the name of an old friend you haven't talked to in a while, or maybe a reminder to get in touch with someone or follow through on a project.

The world before your eyes is as your perceptions tell you it is. The same experience is different for each one of us because each perception is different. As a collective consciousness we each hold to certain realities that make it so. This is not science fiction. You create your own reality, literally. What you see, how you see the world with your eyesight, can change in a single blink. If you are willing to look within and examine your belief systems, experience your inner "gut feelings," you can train yourself to use your insight to improver your eyesight.

Developing insight takes practice. Most of us jump right to our head to calculate what is happening rather than turn within. A TV show recently discussed miracles that happened to people because they had "that feeling" and they trusted it. The choice they made to not walk down a certain street or to call a friend was right on. This is not something that happens sometimes or for others; it can and is happening to you. Pay attention to it. Your insight is a valuable and powerful tool. Learn to use your insight to improve your eyesight.

A Healthy Spiritual Heart

Are you taking care of your Spiritual heart or are you heading for a Spiritual heart attack?

As we become educated in the ways we can live healthier lives by consciously caring for our physical heart, it is equally important to be educated about taking care of our Spiritual heart. The physical and the Spiritual heart are linked together as one in mind, body and spirit. Many believe humans are the connection between heaven and earth. We are the only warm-blooded mammals with our heart exposed because we walk upright on two legs, while all others walk on four legs protecting their hearts. Caring for our Spiritual heart can in turn make our physical heart healthier.

What is the Spiritual heart? Some say the spiritual heart is the link to our soul. As a healthy physical heart keeps our body alive, a healthy spiritual heart keeps our spirit alive. The Spiritual heart has wisdom, an intelligence that knows the broader perspective of our life's purpose. The Spiritual heart feels the emotions. It connects us to our passions, our heart's desires. The Spiritual heart gives our lives purpose and meaning.

The Spiritual heart operates much the same way as the physical heart. Both beat on their own, without us having to think about it. The electrical impulses of the physical heart constantly manage the heartbeat, exercising the heart muscles so life giving blood is cleansed and pumped through our bodies. The electrical impulses of the spiritual heart are constantly opening us up to the wisdom of our spirit, circulating the energy of our emotions and guiding us to live life with a deeper, richer purpose. When the physical heart becomes out of sync or when there are blocks in the passage ways, a heart attack occurs.

What do we do to prevent physical heart attacks? We strengthen the heart muscle by exercising to increase the pulse rate and follow this with relaxation. We eat foods that keep the passages open and flowing. The same is true for preventing a spiritual heart attack. We can strengthen the heart muscle by practicing meditation, prayer or quiet time, making the mind, body, spirit connection. The "food" that keeps the spiritual heart channels open is the feelings and sensations we feel as these emotions surface. If we block our feelings and don't allow them to surface, it will cause a "blockage" in our spiritual heart, much the way blockages occur in our physical heart when we don't properly care for it. Asking the Spiritual heart to cleanse the judgment, anger and resentment helps us feel more compassionate and loving.

Most importantly, when our channels are open, we are able to stay conscious and open to follow the wisdom and guidance of the Spiritual heart. This in turn gives us the courage to take the steps necessary to express the True Nature of our Divine Self. Practicing these physical and mental exercises on a daily basis will lead to a healthier, happier life physically, emotionally and spiritually.

What Were You Thinking?

Has someone ever asked you this question? "What were you thinking?" Or perhaps you asked it of yourself. Most likely this question came at a time when you were experiencing something that you didn't want to experience. And your immediate reactive answer may have been, "I guess I wasn't thinking." This would be followed by some belittling name calling about how stupid or dumb or thoughtless you were.

Now that we are beginning to learn and understand how the Universal Law of Attraction works in our life, we know the answer is not in declaring that you weren't thinking. Instead, take an honest look, without judgment, at what you *were* thinking that created what you did not want. Then, in shifting your awareness, you become empowered to change your thoughts to create more of what you do want to experience.

What is showing up in your life right now? Who are the people in your life? What is your financial status? How are you doing in the pursuit of your new career, your new home? Take an inventory of your life right now. This is the clue to what you WERE thinking!

You are the creator of your reality. The Universal Law of Attraction is always and in all ways working in your life to bring to you the energy of your thoughts. So, what were you thinking?

See something you don't want? Something you are tired of experiencing over and over? Want some situation to come to a close, or to change? Identify what you *were* thinking that brought you what you didn't want, then make a shift in your thoughts and feelings to create more of what you want.

So name it. What is it that you want? What situations do you want to experience? What can you imagine you would be thinking, if you were in the perfect situation, having the perfect experience? From that place of experiencing what you want, what are you thinking, what are you feeling? Now, begin to think and feel as if you are there. Think from that place. Make your actions come from that place.

Take time to really get inside your vision. Imagine the best possible outcome that you want to experience. Practice throughout the day expanding yourself into this new experience. Create the visions, create the energy of your desires and let them shift your energy, and pull you forward.

Then the next time someone says to you, "What were you thinking?" You'll know exactly what it was and make your shift accordingly.

Aligning With Your Vision

When you begin to practice the art of deliberately creating your life, it is very important to align yourself with your desired outcome. This can be done several ways.

You can use the tool of imagination to visualize your desired outcome for a situation, a vacation, or an event you would like to experience. As you close your eyes and imagine the life you desire, take some time to engage all your senses.

Look around you and **SEE** what's in the image you are visualizing. Really see what's in the picture before you. Turn your focus from side to side to get the entire panoramic view. Fully take in the colors and textures. If there are others around you, what do they look like? Reach out and **TOUCH** something or someone in your vision. Pick up an object. What does it feel like? How does it make **you** feel? Exhale deeply. What's the **SMELL** in the air? Perhaps you smell the scent of flowers, or the saltiness of the ocean, or maybe the warm aroma of bread baking? Now tune into what you're hearing, **LISTEN**. The sound of the ocean waves crashing or lapping against the shoreline, the excitement of the audience applauding, the rise and fall of your partner's breath as they lie next to you, or is it simply the stillness and serenity of peace and quiet you hear?   Is there a **TASTE** to your vision? Maybe the essence of the meal you ate earlier, the mint aftertaste in your mouth or the drink of water you just swallowed. Savor it.

Now imagine yourself beginning your day on a crisp autumn morning sitting on the deck of your house in the woods. You may see tall trees surrounding your property and smell the faint sent of pine in the air. Your senses catch the sweetness from the planters of brightly colored flowers in the corners of the deck and you hear the trickling of the water in the fish pond. You feel the softness of your favorite old sweatshirt touching your skin as the breeze gently moves the wind chimes. You taste your first sip of hot coffee or herbal tea as you sit on the deck chair to begin your day with quiet contemplation.

Now take your thought or vision and bring it into reality and "real time" as much as you can. This means you must "think outside the box". For example, if the above vision is what you desire to create and you currently live in an apartment in the city, you can begin aligning and bring your vision into reality several ways. Get up in the morning and have a place where you can sit quietly to contemplate your day. Maybe use a deck chair. Play a CD that has trickling water and wind chimes. Place a few flower pots with brightly colored blossoms on the window sills. How about a fish bowl or mini aquarium? Open the window to feel the chilly autumn air or turn on a fan. Burn a pumpkin spice or autumn harvest scented candle. Purposefully enjoy and savor your first sip of a morning beverage. Maybe even make a collage of photographs or magazine images that take you into your vision and hang it on a wall so you can visit your special place often. You'll find that once you engage your imagination, the possibilities are endless.

First create your vision. Then engage your senses in your vision. Then experience as fully as you can in the **NOW** with how you imagine yourself to be when you are actually living your vision.

The real question to be answered is, "What is your purpose for creating your vision?" In the serene image described above, it may be that your job is stressful and you imagine that if you had a time in the morning to connect with your inner sense of peace, you would move through your work day more relaxed and feel less drained at day's end. After taking time to imagine and align yourself with this concept, begin and move throughout your day as if it were so. How would you be feeling emotionally? How would you be responding to the day's events? How would your conversations flow? How would you make your choices?

The closer you align with your vision, the more it becomes your reality. It begins with your ability to believe you can change the here and now--- right now!

Cultivate Your Genius

You were born a genius. The whole world opens to you when you acknowledge and express your genius. Usually we define the word genius in association with someone that possesses extraordinary intellectual power. But originally the word genius meant "a guardian spirit of a person". Using this definition we can evolve the word "genius" into the word "genie," as in the "genie in the bottle". I believe that each one of us has an extraordinary power that is unique to us, that is the spirit of us. There are no two people alike and when we cultivate our genius, we release our genie out of its bottle and life suddenly becomes awesome.

How do you cultivate your genius? Begin by investing your energy in celebrating you. Stop comparing yourself to others. When you are critical in a negative way, you will always be able to find someone better than you. Keep in mind, this is only your opinion. It's the judgments based on your own perception. Instead of using your energy to see where you are on the ladder of life, use your energy to assume your place in the circle of life. Begin by identifying your skills and talents.

The next question I usually hear is, "What are my skills and talents? I don't know." Stop playing dumb; that doesn't serve anyone. You DO know.

You may not recognize your talents and skills because they are natural and come easily for you. When you express them, you feel energized. It is silly for you to believe that everyone else in the world was sent here with a talent but you. Or that everyone else is blessed with the same particular skills that you enjoy and benefit from which in essence minimizes your skills. Or the Universe gave you something you hate to do as your talent! Now really, I assure you that the Universe does not play that game. So give it up.

Give your skills a space to grow. Choose a job or career that uses your talents. Not only will it be rewarding, but also it will give you a place to cultivate your genius.

- If your genius is being great with details, find a job that cultivates your genius for details.

- If your genius is networking, find a job that cultivates your genius for networking.

- If your genius is leadership, find a job that cultivates your genius for leadership.

- If your genius is encouraging others, find a job that cultivates your genius for encouraging others.

- If your genius is creativity, find a job that cultivates your genius for creativity.

- If your genius is nurturing, find a job that cultivates your genius for nurturing.

- If your genius is organization, find a job that cultivates your genius for organization.

- If your genius is solving problems, find a job that cultivates your genius for solving problems.

- If your genius is teaching, find a job that cultivates your genius for teaching.

- If your genius is having fun, find a job that cultivates your genius for having fun.

- If your genius is entertaining, find a job that cultivates your genius for entertaining.

My latest favorite quote:
"The Universe is not going to see someone like you again in the entire history of creation."
Vartan Gregorian

You have a beautiful skill and talent that is uniquely yours, your natural inclination. Use it for the good of all. When cultivated, it will bring you joy and pleasure. It will keep you feeling young and alive. Others will notice, benefit and enjoy you. They will invite you to share your talent even more. When you accept that your talent is alive and well and you begin to share it, you will be absolutely amazed by your life. The joy and happiness that will grow inside you will align you with the people, places and situations where your talent is needed.

You are a genius. Cultivate it.
There is a place in the world for you.
Find it. Discover it. Share it. Shine it.

Living Your Practice

Broken Promises

Most of the promises we break are the promises we make to ourselves. In some cases, broken promises can become almost "second nature" in the sense that we fail to realize the seriousness of the problem. Take a minute to think about the promises you made to yourself this week and have already broken. Remember the day you committed to "no more sweets", then a co-worker celebrated their birthday with a delicious cake from your favorite bakery? How could you possibly hurt everyone's feelings by not celebrating with the rest of the gang? You couldn't, so you indulged! Remember that promise you made to yourself about not putting any additional purchases on your charge account until you paid off the already too high balance? Then there was the "too good to refuse" once-a-year-sale at your favorite high-end clothing store? How could you pass up a fabulous new outfit at that price? You couldn't, so you bought it! The power of rationalization has become an all too familiar tool for justifying our choices--good or bad.

We may not consciously realize when we rationalize our behavior to make ourselves feel okay, our integrity suffers. Rationalization is the tool we use to convince ourselves that our actions were "not that bad" if we've deviated from our original plan. Try this exercise whenever you find yourself rationalizing: envision a big red flag signaling that you are "out of integrity." The more self-aware we are of our actions, the more we expand our consciousness. As a result, we are called upon more often to play a bigger role in the world. Staying aligned and "living in integrity" is key. We have a responsibility to our core values for the greater good of all.

Integrity means a firm adherence to a code of values. It is not easy living totally and fully aligned with the values we establish for ourselves, yet it is very important we create a firm, clear "base of integrity" and make our choices from this core base. Most of us would say we are committed to telling the truth, keeping our promises, respecting others as well as ourselves and to arrive each day fully prepared for life. And yet, we often compromise ourselves, our personal value and, our integrity when we make choices based on the fear of disappointing someone else.

When we base our life on pleasing others, we create entangled, confusing relationships. Lines of communication become blurred, resulting in misunderstandings and misinterpretations. The more out of alignment we become with our true self, the more our emotions become buried or exaggerated. Life becomes more and more challenging and less and less satisfying. We become resentful and mentally exhausted, yet we can't really explain why. When we don't feel good about ourselves, our life's situations and the people around us, we feel drained and confused. Our "life force energy" supply quickly becomes depleted.

Living in integrity
Life is "energy in motion." When we live in integrity and align ourselves with a higher awareness of the Self, our energy flows freer. We become more authentic and live life as dynamic and powerful human beings. Our inner alignment is reflected in our outer affairs. In essence, we reflect what we project. We feel good about ourselves and others feel good about us. When we live in integrity, our energy flows with more abundance. We are more in tune with our intuition; we hear the inner voice as the voice of our Higher Self. It speaks over the "mind rationalizing" voice. We are better able to use discernment in our interactions and dealings with others. Others respect us because we respect ourselves. They

get a "good feeling" about us. Instead of viewing problems as negative obstacles, we embrace them as opportunities. It becomes easier for us to call on creativity when we need the perfect solution to any given situation.

Take responsibility

Life changes when we become clear about our priorities and take responsibility to align ourselves on the inside with our core values. We are more fully integrated in mind, body and spirit. Our energy becomes more clear and powerful. We are aware of our emotions and know how to consciously "feel" our feelings and express them appropriately, rather than express them on reactionary or pent up emotion and frustration. We let go of regrets, shame and guilt about our actions. Worry, fear and anxiety lessen as we release the need to manipulate the world. Our communications become clearer and are expressed purposefully because we are confident, clear and focused in our intentions. We become better listeners, validating others' perceptions and feelings without judgment or criticism because we have less filters analyzing words, tone and body language. We connect with others more intimately because we are more connected intimately with ourselves.

Making apologies

When life feels out of control, let it be a signal that somewhere you are "out of integrity." When you arrive late for an appointment or forget to return a phone call, offer your sincere apology and quickly clear the air. "I apologize" is enough said. There is no need to explain, rationalize, and make excuses or promise to do better the next time. When you make an agreement and fail to follow through you change your energy flow. When you rationalize or make excuses you further change the flow of your energy and begin to create a tangled web around you. Stop, take a moment to reflect and make any necessary adjustments. When there is a birthday party at work, celebrate fully but pass on the cake. Believe me, a month later no one is going to remember you didn't eat cake at their party! Remove yourself from the temptation to "just look" at the mall when you're committed to having manageable debt. Trust me; the store will be there ready and willing to accept your money when you're ready!

Living in integrity sets a new pace for our lives. When we tell the truth, keep our promises and respect ourselves we align with integrity. Our energy begins to flow like a smooth, tranquil river with life's beauty thriving all around us. We feed others by giving freely from our infinite inner resource. As we raise our consciousness, we raise the consciousness of others. We love more because we are loved more. Living in integrity changes our entire outlook on life. Make a promise to yourself to live in integrity each and every day. It's a promise worth keeping.

Developing Inner Core Strength

I was introduced to the Pilates Method of exercise a few years ago and have since been fascinated with the idea of "core strengthening". The Pilates exercise program consists of a series of movements designed to strengthen the core of your body by working on targeted areas. The exercises tone, reshape and firm you up with a simple yet very effective technique. Investing just 15 minutes a day in the Pilates Method can make a difference in how you feel and relate to your physical body. As a Life/Spiritual Coach, I have been considering ways in which to design a life exercises program that strengthen the inner-core of who we are as individuals from an emotional and spiritual standpoint.

Our inner-core consists of the principles and values by which we live. The more we develop these inner-core strengths, the more we raise our personal awareness and spiritual self-esteem. I believe these two areas of life are related. As we feel good about our personal self, we express the Spirit of Life more fully. When we strengthen our inner core, we have better posture in the way we walk through life. We become more flexible in the way we handle life's situations. We move gracefully through challenges. We base our choices around what we believe, and stay focused on what we know is true.

I learned a lot as I researched Joseph Pilates and I believe his inner-core strength supported him in creating this method of physical exercise. There was a calling in his soul he heard and followed. Before he was 14 years old, he studied anatomy and ancient exercise regimes of the Greeks and Romans. He also studied yoga and Zen meditation. He went to great lengths and made life choices by what was in his heart as he followed his soul's calling. He defined his technique as "complete coordination of body, mind and spirit." The strength of his inner-core guided him in developing the Pilates Method of exercise.

When imprisoned during WWI, Joseph Pilates trained his fellow inmates in his exercises, which helped them to not only survive prison, but a deadly flu epidemic as well. He was then sent to work as a nurse to care for patients who were immobilized by war injuries. While there, he used bed springs and straps hung from the ceiling to teach and develop his program. When asked to train soldiers, he declared his methods were for healing, not harming, and he left Germany. This choice brought him to set up his studio in NYC where he began to train dancers and eventually athletes. Joseph Pilates is a real testimony of someone who allowed his adversity and the strength of his inner-core call him to a higher purpose.

Exercises that strengthen your spiritual and emotional inner-core:
- Observe Self-Talk – train yourself to say kind and loving words to yourself.
- Contemplate what you believe – create a list of what you know is true.
- When asked to make a choice, do so consciously.
- Spend 15 minutes a day in quiet inner connection and meditation.

Turning Confrontations into Conversations

Few of us look forward to confrontation. When we have "issues" with someone our energy has become strained or "jammed up". We often feel the energy between us and this person has become a battleground and confronting them feels like we're heading into battle. And as with any battleground, we have to arm and protect ourselves in anticipation of war. In any war there will be a winner and a loser. War-like confrontations often involve each side yelling and screaming to be heard, with each person taking the "I am right, and I want to be sure you know that I am right" attitude. We don't go into a confrontation looking for a win-win solution; we each want to come out the winner. Trust me when I say, confrontations never work for anyone.

We must also take into consideration conflicts are unavoidable and arise on a daily basis. Each one of us is "a bundle of beliefs and opinions" that at times differs from someone else's "bundles of beliefs and opinions". It is important to call on our internal wisdom to guide us in knowing which conflicts to let go of, which to walk away from and which ones are important enough to have a conversation about. If you are willing to have a conversation with someone before the battle arises, you increase the possibility of a win/win solution.

Here are 4 steps to having a peaceful conversation:

1. Have the conversation as soon as possible after the conflict arises.
The longer you wait, the more the splinter will fester and you'll begin to leak energy. Each day that goes by without discussing it with the other person builds up more tension and conflict. You may even begin to have arguments

127

about the situation in your own head, building your case for being right. In these conversations you will project the other person's perspective about the conflict perhaps even making up what they are thinking, feeling and saying. Having the conversation as soon as possible after the conflict stops this insanity.

2. Take on the attitude that you are not "right" about this situation.
Both you and the other person have different perceptions and opinions to which each is entitled. Be open to listening to their point of view. Know that their point of view is just as real to them as your point of view is to you. Agree that you each have different perceptions. Once they feel acknowledged, they will be more apt to listen to your point of view. The road to resolution is not a one-way street.

3. Take a moment to get clear on what you want to express.
Enter into the conversation believing that you will hear and be heard and that each of you will eventually get to a place of understanding each other's position. Each of you wants, and deserves, to be heard and validated. What is true for you is also true for the other person. Getting clear means that you stay within the topic of the conflict not bringing any other past issues into the conversation.

4. Before the conversation, sit quietly, move into your heart space and envision the outcome you desire.
See you and the other person having a great conversation, each listening to the other's perception, shaking hands and both of you feeling like you've been victorious. Even if that means that you agree to disagree and respect each other's perception. Listening, validating and respecting each other in itself can resolve the conflict.

And let's face it, there are people in this world who walk around so afraid of appearing vulnerable and weak that they see most situations as a "fight to be right," or a "battle to be won." When you come in conflict with such a person, have the wisdom to walk away. No conversations will ever be heard except the one inside you, with your inner guide encouraging you to "walk away from this one," and "send this person love," because they sure could use an extra dose right now.

Be inspired this week to let go of the conflict. Ask your inner wisdom which conversations are yours to have. Ask for the courage to listen, validate and speak your truth. Believe in a win/win solution. Peace on earth happens as we individually clear our personal conflicts.

Time For an Emotional Alignment?

Whenever you get new tires on your car, they always ask if you want them aligned. Having the wheels, tires and the vehicle aligned properly makes the car run more efficient. As a result of an alignment, you get the best use, most mileage and a smoother ride from your vehicle. This same theory can be applied to your emotions. When you are aligned with emotions that are open, loving, connecting and expanding, you get the best value and smoother ride through life's journey.

Emotions are silent "body language"; giving us a read on the people, places and situations we encounter throughout the day. Each one of us is constantly reading the "energy" of the world around us. Life itself is energy in motion. We, as human beings, are energy in "real time". The way we direct our energy and put it into motion is through our emotions. Emotions are "**E**-nergy in **MOTION**."

Emotions are neither good nor bad. How we invest ourselves in life is directed by our emotions. Emotions range from fearful to loving. Many books have been written about emotional intelligence, the wisdom of emotions and expressing emotional maturity. The more consciously we live, the more aware we become and the more responsible we are for aligning ourselves with loving emotions. When we realize and experience the benefits of living consciously, we feel more alive and in tune with ourselves. Therefore, it begins to become second nature.

Fearful emotions cause us to judge, blame, attack, worry, become anxious and feel separated from others and create more fear within ourselves. Some fearful emotions are:

- Resentment
- Regret
- Competition
- Fear
- Worry
- Anxiety
- Sadness

Fear, anger and resentment are restricting emotions that cause us to tighten up physically, mentally and emotionally. They cause us create blinders and limit our vision. Remember a time when you were angry about something and how tense you became? Anger is a low frequency emotion because it is restrictive and tight. Breathing becomes shallow and may create an actual physical tightness in our chest. You may remember that when you held on to that anger for a long period of time, things went from bad to worse. By staying in anger, you aligned yourself with fear. You put the energy of your life in alignment with anger and you attracted more situations to make you angry. Take a moment to really consider the power of that concept. You'll see it's true.

Loving emotions cause us to be empathetic, kind, joyful, compassionate and feel connected to others, which cause more love in our experiences. Some loving emotions are:
- Joy
- Love
- Happiness
- Compassion
- Gentleness
- Gratitude
- Kindness

Love, compassion and joy are expanding emotions that allow us to feel open, relaxed and calm mentally, physically and emotionally. Remember a time when you felt deep joy and excitement about something that happened to you? Maybe a new job, a windfall of money, or perhaps you fell in love. The frequency of love is high. Love opens you up. Did you feel like you could do anything? Did you feel a lightness and connection to everyone around you? Did you feel open and receptive to life? Did you attract people and situations that made you feel more love?

We cannot always be aligned with love of course. I am not telling you to deny your emotions if they are fearful. Denial leads to building barriers and eventually creates more anger. I am suggesting that you become more conscious and more aware of your emotions and really **feel** and **experience** them. You choose which frequency of emotions to align yourself with. When fearful things happen, love yourself and feel the fear, but release the fear in safe, healthy and constructive ways instead of putting yourself in unhealthy or destructive situations. When you do this, you'll find a segue into love.

Getting an emotional alignment allows you to experience life in a healthy, positive manner; creating mental, emotional and physical balance. Think of it this way, after the alignment, your car ran much more smoothly, gave you a comfortable and pleasant ride and most importantly, it created peace of mind within you. Why not make the same emotional investment in yourself? When you are emotionally aligned with love, you get better mileage from life!

Turning Speed-Bumps,
Roadblocks and Detours Into "Signals"

Remember the last time you took a road trip? With your bags packed, car loaded, map on the front seat, destination circled, you anxiously anticipated your arrival. Suddenly, you ran into a roadblock and the blaring orange detour signs took you off course. Did the disappointment change your attitude about your well-planned journey? Did you feel frustrated as your "best laid plans" hit a snag?

The same disappointment and frustration can happen to us as we move toward a goal in life. I want to help you reframe the speed bumps, roadblocks and detours that happen in life to empower you to see them as "signals" rather than deterrents.

Speed bumps – A speed bump is a small ridge in the road that limits your speed and cautions you to slow down. When you hit a speed bump on your journey through life, let it be a "signal" that you are to slow down, become aware and pay attention. Maybe there is something you are supposed to notice that will answer a question you've been asking. Maybe you need to be present to receive directions or information you will need to know in the future. Maybe you are the one who has the insight to share with someone else and slowing down to notice them is important.

Roadblocks – A roadblock is a barricade that stops your progress. It often means there is construction or danger ahead. When you hit a roadblock on your journey, let it be a "signal" there is something you need to reconstruct. Maybe you have an old belief that is no longer helpful for you to hold onto. Maybe it's time to clear out the accumulated "stuff" in your life. Maybe your map is outdated and it is time for redirection.

Detours – A detour is a diversion from a direct course. When you are driving and are instructed to follow a detour, you are redirected to your destination. Taking this redirection gives you the opportunity to experience different scenery. When a detour presents itself on your life's journey, let it be a "signal" that you are headed for the perfect destination via a different route. Pay attention to the experiences that come your way. Recognize the synchronicities that happen. Remember you will arrive at your designed destination; you're just getting there by following a different path of direction that wasn't originally in your game plan. Pay attention to the people you meet, the new experiences you have, the "scenery" you see. They all serve a purpose and have a specific reason for being chartered on this new path.

By practicing the technique of reframing, you empower yourself to use all the experiences in life as signposts along the way. When you hit a speed bump, are stopped by a roadblock or are sent on a detour, remember to reframe. Let your frustrations remind you to pay attention to the "signals". Ignoring or fighting against them will throw you even further off course. Listening to these "signals," will cause you to **redirect**, **refocus** and **resume** the right path on your life's journey.

Rituals, Ceremonies and Rites of Passage

Does the word ritual conger up visions of natives dancing wildly around a blazing fire performing some sort of hocus-pocus? Or do you have childhood memories of the rituals performed in your church or temple that you didn't understand or dreaded.

Marion Webster defines the ritual as "to fit together." Celebrating rituals is the way we fit together the metaphysical or unseen world and the physical world. The rituals we are most familiar celebrate the rites of passage created according to various religious laws or social customs.

Christenings, baptisms, and bris celebrate our entrance into the world while Bar /Bat mitzvahs, confirmations and Holy Communions celebrate our coming of age. Birthdays are rituals we celebrate as children and usually not again until when we reach the age that we are grateful to still be alive. Graduations celebrate our accomplishments and entrance into adulthood. Weddings recognize the beginning of a shared life. When death comes we have funerals, memorial celebrations to recognize our leaving this earth. When grandchildren arrive we once again focus our attention on celebrating new life. The time between reaching adulthood and death, the time when we are most conscious about our choices and life's experiences often goes unrecognized and uncelebrated.

When I turned fifty I create a ritual celebration acknowledging my passage through four decades and honoring that I was entering into a new phase of life. I wanted to affirm that I was wiser and clearer about how I wanted to experience life and the contributions I will leave behind. With a few close friends witnessing, I lit candles, one for each decade, while sharing the significant events and the lessons that each taught me. Passing around a variety of glass beads each friend chose one that represented their relationship with me. Stringing her bead, each woman shared its significance.

Rituals can be created to celebrate many occasions and rites of passage. I am often called upon to bless a house, to clear out old energy and acknowledge the new owners and their intentions for creating this house as their home. By creating a ritual celebration thanking the house for the many years and fond memories a friend was able to sell her house in record time.

How about a ritual celebration for a divorce? The process of divorce takes a lot of time and energy. In the end you receive a piece of paper in the mail that often feels anti-climatic. By creating a ritual celebration bringing closure and cutting the ties to that relationship, you bring yourself into present time making yourself available for a new relationship.

The love of friendships can be acknowledged and renewed with a ritual celebration. A new job, retirement or creative ventures are all significant events that call for a ritual celebration. Our journey through life is rich because of the joys and the sorrows. Moving through illness, depression or a stressful time can be honored with a ritual celebration. The last radiation treatment or passing the "three-year mark" is certainly a rite of passage that deserves a ritual celebration.

Rituals can be as simple as lighting a candle while sitting in a room by yourself or as elaborate as your imagination can create. Elements of ritual include intention, space, sequence, ingredients and personal meaning.

Intention - What is most important is your sincerity. Ask yourself what event or situation do you want to recognize? What is your purpose for creating this ritual?

Space - Creating the space is important because it consciously helps focus your attention. This may mean that you houseclean, set a table for a ritual meal or turn your coffee table into an altar.

Sequence - Create a beginning and an ending to your ritual. Ringing a bell, lighting a candle, clap your hands can begin your ritual. Reading a poem, saying a prayer or a moment of silence can create closure.

Ingredients - Your imagination can go wild with this element. Music with special meaning, candles, aromas, flowers and foods brings our senses into the ritual. Journals, photographs and memory books add a significant dimension.

Personal Meaning - Why does celebrating this event have meaning for you? This may be reflected in your silence or your words. If you are celebrating with friends, you may want them to participate by sharing their relationship to you or this event.

By consciously bringing ritual celebrations into our lives we join together mind, body and spirit adding sacredness to everyday life. We help release the anxiety of change, focus our attention, and honor the many rites of passage we come through. Ritual celebrations can help us recognize the wisdom we've gained and the companions we met on our journey through life.

Epilogue

Gracias   Merci   Danke

Grazie   Thank-you

Tada   Ahsante

Gratitude – the Key

To speak gratitude is courteous and pleasant.
To enact gratitude is generous and noble.
To live gratitude is to touch heaven.

Johannes Gaerther

Gratitude is the magic key that can unlock the doors to a rich and abundant life! Gratitude is an attitude we can cultivate that will keep us aware of the many treasures that life offers. Gratitude may seem like a small thing, but it can enrich us beyond measure, helping us experience a more fulfilled life.

Two simple words "thank you", spoken in every language around the world are the easiest way we can express gratitude. As children we were all taught to say "please" and "thank you" as a show of good manners. The United States is the only nation to have signed a declaration setting aside a day of Thanksgiving showing that our founding fathers believed in the power of giving thanks.

Living with an attitude of gratitude can profoundly transform us. When we place our attention on the things we are grateful for, we can walk through life using this tiny key to unlock the doors to a rich and blessed life.

Several years ago Sarah Ben Breathrach, author of "Simple Abundance" appeared on Oprah. Sarah writes about living more authentically and teaches that gratitude

143

is the first step to traveling the path of joy. Together, Sarah and Oprah began a nationwide movement to raise our awareness of the power of gratitude by inviting us to keep a gratitude journal. The assignment was to begin our journal by listing five things we are grateful for every night before we go to bed. Sounds like an easy assignment, right? Here's the challenge. We are asked to give thanks for something different everyday! This means not writing the same thing twice. What a challenging invitation teaching us to really look and to see the tiny gems life offers us day in and day out.

Life is a Divine paradox. When gratitude will help us the most, is when we feel most ungrateful. What we all want most is to feel loved. We can't always control the situations that happen in life, but we can choose how we perceive life's situations. When we perceive life as going "right", we feel loved and connected. We have more confidence in ourselves. We feel lucky. It is easier for us to be kind and generous and to bestow confidence in others at these times.

But, when we perceive life as going "wrong" we feel unloved and disconnected. Complaining, faultfinding and taking what we have for granted shuts us off from what we want most, to feel loved. This is the time we most need to use the key of gratitude to free us from the prison of our minds misperceptions.

As a Holistic Life Coach I use gratitude to empower clients to sole their problems. When clients share with me the challenges in their lives, one of the first things we talk about is their perception of the situation and how that perception makes them feel. We talk about what they believe the answer to this situation would look like, what do they believe needs to happen externally for them to feel more loved and secure internally? Together, we look at how we can change the perception of the situation, how we can be grateful for the gifts seen and unseen offered in the experience. When we can change the internal perception, through acceptance and gratitude, we get back into the flow of life opening ourselves for creative solutions to come forward.

The more we use the key of gratitude we soon realize that giving thanks in before we face a situation is most transforming. Wayne Dyer author of "Manifesting Your Destiny" states the ninth principle for getting everything you want is "Reaching to Your Manifestation with Gratitude and Generosity". In other words, learn to give thanks in advance for what you want to experiences in life. He says it this way; "the nature of gratitude is the complete and full response of the human heart to everything in the universe. It is the absence of feeling separated. It represents our full acknowledgement and appreciation of the energy flowing through all things and brings gifts to us in the form of fulfillment to our desires."

The key of gratitude is a perception; a way of thinking that can become a way of life. It is freely available to each of us. We cultivate gratitude as we learn to stay open, remembering we have a choice in how we perceive life's experiences. Keeping a gratitude journal helps us to focus on giving thanks for what we have received. During the times we feel most ungrateful is when turning the gratitude key is most valuable, giving us the ideal opportunity to give thanks in advance for a solution.

As we transform ourselves we consciously create a more loving, gentler and kinder world. We are offered this key of gratitude, how we put it to use is your choice.

From "Attitude of Gratitude" by M J Ryan

- Gratitude is the mother of joy
- Gratitude makes us feel young
- Gratitude cures perfectionism
- Gratitude is an antidote of bitterness-resentment
- Gratitude draws people to us
- Gratitude eradicates worry
- Gratitude promotes health
- Gratitude makes us feel good
- Gratitude makes us feel young
- Gratitude releases us from the gimmies
- Gratitude opens our heart
- Gratitude spawns kindness and generosity
- Gratitude joins us to all life
- Gratitude connects us to Spirit
- Gratitude opens us to moments of grace

A Personal Note from the Author

I would like to introduce myself and share with you how I came to be able to create this enlightening book for you.

My name is Sharon Marquart. Through synchronistic events in my life, or as Deepak Chopra refers to them, through the "snychrodestiny" of life, I "woke up". I became aware that there is a Divine Self of me and that I had been hypnotized into a "trance of unworthiness" for many years. It was a trance that kept me trapped in an unhealthy body and mind for a very long time. The trance also kept me from being able to see or know "light" or "love". I knew I needed a choice moment, a sense of direction. When I began to come out of the trance and placed value on myself, a new path formed.

I realized that the True Nature of my Divine Self is Love. As I placed my attention on Love, staying awake to Love, I began my healing journey. This journey showed me the walls and blocks I had built around me that kept me in a state of hypnotized unworthiness. Discovering Love changed all of that. For more than 18 years, I have been journeying with Love as my guide and am more at peace physically, emotionally and spiritually than I have ever been.

In 1996 I was inspired (in-spirited) to create Open Heart Ministries. I soon realized its acronym, OHM, is the name for God. As I grew, Open Heart Ministries began to take on a life of its own. At OHM, I created workshops, lectures and classes to share the teachings that Love gave me, and the stories of my healing. I began coaching others and holding the space for them to make their healing journey. OHM has created many ways for me to inspire others to wake up and remember Love is the foundation which guides us all through life. How we choose to use it in our lives means the difference between living an empty life or a life of abundance.

In 2004 I was inspired by the phrase, "Living at YES!" A slogan, when kept in mind, reminds you to choose Love, to say, "YES!" to live. I was in-spirited to call "Living at YES!" into being. The acronym YES means **Y**OU **E**MBRACING **S**PIRIT.

What is "Living at YES!"?

"Living at Yes!" means living fully as our unique selves, embracing and accepting our spiritual natures. "Living at Yes!" is about bringing heaven to earth as the human part of us embraces and reflects the spiritual or soulful part of us. I believe that as each individual evolves personally, we raise the energy of the earth to a higher level. The physical plane of existence and the Spiritual plane of existence begin to merge into one.

I will take a few moments to briefly share my beliefs about life. I think that the ultimate is Oneness of life. Meaning that in the Spiritual sense, in the invisible form of Spirit, we are all connected. I have several beliefs on how and why we are individualized but that could take an entire book to explain, so I'll just say I believe that we have individualized on planet earth for the purpose of seeing beyond our separated selves, joining all together in one Spirit. This is truly bringing heaven to earth, the ultimate "Peace on Earth". *There will be peace on earth when we can see beyond our differences and know that we are all the same at our core.*

"Living at YES!" is sharing what is in our heart and doing what we can to bring peace on earth. When the collective consciousness of humanity reaches a pivotal number of us aware of our oneness, we will change the world.

What Does Living at "You Embracing Spirit" Look Like?

It can look very different for each of us. Throughout this book I have included stories from my life and members of the "Living at YES!" community in order to share how our lives have evolved by using the four principles. "Living at YES!" supports you living your best life now. When you live more consciously, you have a vision of who you are and your place in the circle of life. You realize your presence makes a difference in the world. You experience freedom because you know how to make empowering choices. The vision of your life is expansive and your heart is opened to share hope, joy, love and compassion with others.

How Do You "Live at YES!"?

To "Live at YES!" means that you are clear on the purpose of your life. This does not mean that you won't have ups and downs occasionally, we all do. It means that you are utilizing the "4 Principles" identified here in your life. It means that you are grateful for what is in your life now and what you desire to experience. It means that you are able to imagine the endless possibilities for your life. It means that your beliefs are based on healthy choices and that the choices you make are empowering to you.

To Find Out More About Sharon and "Living at YES!"

I encourage you to visit the "Living at YES!" web site at http://www.livingatyes.com for a full schedule of classes and events. On the web site you will find inspiring products, including a line of custom-designed T-shirts, coffee mugs, mouse pads, and more. These products were created to serve as a reminder for you to stay conscious and focused in the moment at any given point during the day.

In addition to personal coaching and being a keynote speaker at various functions throughout the United States, I teach international tele-classes, conduct free monthly tele-classes and lead community calls here you can join with others of like mind and declare your intentions as you consciously learn to create your life. I currently travel throughout the United States as a keynote motivational speaker, teacher and life coach. If you want to learn more about how you can become a happier and healthier you, I am available to new clients. I offer a complimentary introductory session to see if my style of coaching is right for you.

I hope you enjoy reading this book and allow it to serve as a guide as you Embrace the Spirit of Life. Remember, LIFE is a gift to be lived in full abundance.

With an Open Heart,

Sharon Marquart
Living at YES!